MIND MAPPING

How Easy It Is to Retain More Information

(Navigate Your Thoughts Methodically With Digital Mind Maps)

Sabrina Brown

Published By Sabrina Brown

Sabrina Brown

All Rights Reserved

Mind Mapping: How Easy It Is to Retain More Information (Navigate Your Thoughts Methodically With Digital Mind Maps)

ISBN 978-1-77485-434-1

All rights reserved. No part of this guide may be reproduced in any form without permission in writing from the publisher except in the case of brief quotations embodied in critical articles or reviews.

Legal & Disclaimer

The information contained in this book is not designed to replace or take the place of any form of medicine or professional medical advice. The information in this book has been provided for educational and entertainment purposes only.

The information contained in this book has been compiled from sources deemed reliable, and it is accurate to the best of the Author's knowledge; however, the Author cannot guarantee its accuracy and validity and cannot be held liable for any errors or omissions. Changes are periodically made to this book. You must consult your doctor or get professional medical advice before using any of the suggested remedies, techniques, or information in this book.

Upon using the information contained in this book, you agree to hold harmless the Author from and against any damages, costs, and expenses, including any legal fees potentially resulting from the application of any of the information provided by this guide. This disclaimer applies to any damages or injury caused by the use and application, whether directly or indirectly, of any advice or information presented, whether for breach of contract, tort, negligence, personal injury, criminal intent, or under any other cause of action.

You agree to accept all risks of using the information presented inside this book. You need to consult a professional medical practitioner in order to ensure you are both able and healthy enough to participate in this program.

TABLE OF CONTENTS

INTRODUCTION 1

CHAPTER 1: THE WRITER'S BLOCK 3

CHAPTER 2: ORGANIZE YOUR THOUGHTS 9

CHAPTER 3: TYPES AND EXAMPLES OF MIND MAPPING .. 12

CHAPTER 4: WHAT IS MIND MAPPING ANYWAY? 31

CHAPTER 5: MIND MAPPING TIPS AND STRATEGIES 46

CHAPTER 6: HOW THE HUMAN BRAIN LEARNS 56

CHAPTER 7: EDUCATION MADE EASIER WITH MIND MAPPING 71

CHAPTER 8: VISUAL MAPPING METHODS & TYPES 90

CHAPTER 9: OPTIMIZING 6 MEETINGS 107

CHAPTER 10: FEELINGS CAN SOMETIMES BE THE MOST POWERFUL BUT ALSO THE MOST DETRIMENTAL ASPECT OF LIFE. 124

CHAPTER 11: EXERCISES 142

CHAPTER 12: UTILIZE MIND MAPS 149

CHAPTER 13: MIND MAPPING PRECAUTIONS 160

CONCLUSION 177

Introduction

In these pages, I will demonstrate how mind mapping can be used to improve your life. This book can help you improve your studies, plan for projects, or organize your home and 'to-do' lists.

Mind maps and mind mapping can be the best way to organize information. Because you can see everything in one spot, your brain will retain details better due to the visual nature. Mind maps are a great way to improve your project management and learning.

However, it can be challenging to get the art of mind-mapping down to the best way to help you. This is why I wrote the book. To help eliminate any confusion in creating useful and effective mindmaps, it was essential that you have a clear understanding of how to do it.

Mastering mind mapping will help you improve your learning, concentration, memory, organization and problem solving skills.

Everything in this book can be understood in a straightforward, simple and easy-to-follow manner. I cover everything from basic mind mapping to advanced techniques which will greatly improve your workflow.

You'll be able organize your life more effectively after reading this book. If you know how to use a Mind Map correctly, you will be able to organize everything you need.

Chapter 1: The Writer's Block

In this chapter, we'll be focusing our attention on writer's block. The writer's bloc is when you feel stuck. This can lead to a slowdown in your writing and even a halt to the completion of your work. We must prevent this from happening and cure ourselves of the condition. Here are some tips for how to get rid.

Do something artistic. Try something new. Your creativity can be satisfied by the activities you enjoy. If you love to dance, turn up your volume and put on your favorite song. Make your favorite dish if you love cooking. If you love to draw and paint, grab your sketchpads or canvass and spend some time with your favorite activity. For whatever reason, it doesn't matter what you love about art or writing. Instead of writing, put down your pen and go do something creative for a while.

Freewriting. You can also freewrite if you really are stuck with what you are writing. Set your timer for a couple of minutes and get started writing. It doesn't matter if your grammatical accuracy, punctuation marks or handwriting are correct. You can just write. Write whatever comes to your mind and tell the story. Write about what happened yesterday, whereabouts, and people with whom you've been. Write on until the alarm goes off. This can be done daily, every other week or as a part of your daily routine. This not only keeps you creative, but the ideas that you write can be an inspiration for what you are writing about. You might even get new ideas to add into your article or book.

Move. Stop sitting in your office chair looking at the blank pages for too many hours. Get up and get moving. Sing along to your favorite song. Do your workout. Go for a jog, or run. Do activities that activate your body. If your body is active your brain will too. The brain becomes more active, and your brain will begin to produce more creative ideas.

Start early. You'll be in that creative stage when you wake-up. If you want to start your day early, start it with your mindmap.

It will help you not only get your tasks done quickly but also make it easy for you to create one. Some people rise at 5 in morning while others rise at noon. Whatever time you wake-up, get started by making a mindmap or going back to the place you were last writing.

You should think of your problem as a problem before you fall asleep. If you're stuck in your mind map or in a specific chapter of your novel then you will soon be unable to move on. Your problem, or the part that is preventing you from moving forward, can be thought of as your sleeping problems. Because while you are asleep, your subconscious thoughts about your problem will continue to haunt you. As a result, dreams can often be your solution. And when you wake up, your brain may still have some clues that will help you continue your work. Consider your problem as you lay in bed. When you wake up, you'll have a solution.

Restore your energy and let it go. You can rest and relax if you're too tired to work. Scientists have also confirmed that getting enough sleep improves brain function and creativity. You may have been up all night and have not been getting enough sleep. This will make it more difficult to accomplish even the simplest tasks. Take a step back and have a good rest or take a nap if you need to get your deadline done. Give yourself a break if you don't get enough sleep or you feel like you can't express your creativity and are stressed. You can try to relax by taking a deep, slow breath and letting your head clear a little. Relaxing allows you to let your mind open, allowing you to be more creative.

Keep a pencil and paper on hand. If you find yourself stuck and need to take a break, remember to keep a pen and paper handy so that you can capture any creative ideas. Keep a pen & paper handy when you go to the gym. Always be prepared to record your thoughts and take notes right then.

Give yourself a meal. Take care of you health. When your body is in top shape, your mind will follow it. Take care of your health and never skip meals. Get started each morning with a healthy breakfast. You can eat different foods. You should eat in moderation and eat a variety of foods. Science has proven that eating well can affect your brain function. Don't be afraid to eat when you are hungry. Hydration is key.

Listen and read. Writing is hard work. If this happens, there are more lessons that can be learned to help you find new inspiration and ideas. The daily newspaper, Hollywood and Celebrity News, magazines you love, and even the most scientific books you like, are all good places to start. Reading allows you to not only gain knowledge about the subject they have covered but also helps expand your vocabulary and improve your writing abilities. You might find new ideas to add to your writing. Talk to people. They might have something to share that you won't find in your regular reading. Listen to their stories, challenges and how you dealt with them. Do not be afraid of asking questions to get the information you require.

It encourages creativity and can help you prevent writer's blocking. Along with focusing on ways to prevent writer's block, it is important that you start making your ideamap and making it memorable.

Chapter 2: Organize Your Thoughts

Your thoughts and ideas must be organized. It is important to organize these thoughts. Organization requires consistency and discipline. If you forget to do one thing, it is easy for everything else to go wrong. While this may seem like a tedious task, it is vital to your success.

Tip 1 Always Keep a Notebook with You for Notes

This seems pretty straightforward, right? The truth is, it is not. There are many factors that could cause you to forget to take a notebook and a pencil. Laziness can be one of the reasons. The notebook you carry will make it seem like a waste of time. You can still remember what you need and will have one less thing to carry. You are just being lazy! As we have found, writing things down is far more efficient than using notes apps. Always carry a pencil and a notepad. You won't regret. It's better than to be safe than sorry.

Tip 2 Separate ideas that are for short-term goals from ideas for long-term goals

Now that your ideas have been written down and are easily remembered, it's important to distinguish between short-term goals and long-term goals. Why? This will help you be more efficient. It is best to stay focused on the ideas that must be used first, and ignore ideas that may not be used yet. This will make it easier to not get lost. You'll finish tasks faster by focusing on what is happening now.

Tip 3 Categorize and Organize Your Thoughts According To Topic

Everybody has limits, both mentally as well as physically. It is impossible to do everything at once. It is almost impossible. It is vital to properly categorize all ideas and thoughts. There are different times throughout the day for work, leisure, hobbies and even for family members. It will help you be more productive in your use of thoughts and ideas by categorizing them. For example, when you are at work, your focus will be on the work related ideas. This improves productivity.

Tip 4 Make lists

Another way to use your notebook is to make lists and organize your thoughts. Once you've sorted your thoughts by topic and have identified the priorities, you are ready to make lists. As I mentioned before, physical reminders help to improve focus and memory. As an example, consider the work example. It is much more productive and efficient to take down all the details and make lists. This will help you build character and discipline, which can help in many things.

Chapter 3: Types And Examples Of Mind Mapping

Brain maps are often used in daily life and work. Therefore, everyone should be aware of the main types of thoughts map so that they can make a decision on which one to use. Mind maps can generally be divided into three types based on the purpose of use: library thoughtmaps, demonstration mindmaps, and tube deadline thoughtmaps. We'll get into more detail about them later.

Both designers and nondesigners often use mindmaps to brainstorm ideas in the initial stages of jobs. In an earlier article we looked at mind maps and how they can be used. Mind maps are created by starting with a core thought and growing it into a structure. Tree structures allow you to link thoughts together and give more information. Mind maps can either be created using paper or a board. You can also use post-it sticky note or other online tools. Our mind map template is designed to be printed and can be used for creating flexible brain maps.

It is essential to know the difference between different types and what they are for. This will help you create a productive mind-mapping session. There are three basic types of brainmaps that can be used depending on the purpose of the project: library thoughtmaps to monitor data, demo mindmaps to present thoughts and tube timeline thoughtmaps to help with organizing and building a strategy. This taxonomy covers the goal of mindmaps as well as the information that was used in the brainstorming session.

Mind maps are often used at the beginning phase of a project to find out more about the topic and resolve any problems. Mind maps could be divided into 3 types according to their function.

The library head map is for organizing advice

The presentation thought channels are for job and idea presentations

You can create or modify a job strategy using tunnel deadline thinking maps

Mind Map Form 1: Library Mind maps

Reference maps are also known to library mind maps. This type of mind map is used to organize the information in order to be able to understand the issue clearly without missing any details. Library thought maps were created to make it easier for users to understand and organize the collected information.

Library mindmaps, also known by the reference map, are used to organize information visually. Many pieces of advice can be viewed at once without having any loss. This mind map starts off with a few broken thoughts or topics, then these thoughts are combined into a tree structure. This arrangement can help to build a connection between related thoughts, and arrange the best topics. The library map centers on the idea. It begins with the most fundamental thought. Then it guides brainstorming by following the subjects to the center ideas.

The first step after creating a library brain map is to organize all information and make a map shrub. The map will show you how each piece is connected to the others and how they could be used together to serve the principle thought.

This kind of mindmap may be used to organize information on a subject in visual form. Below are a few examples: mind map personal profile

This may be possible by using the library brain map:

Find out more about a topic or the ideas that surround it. To illustrate, this can be used by a team to research a topic such as traffic lights and the associated issues so that it can be resolved.

Visually organize information about one job or subject. You can track it during the conversation.

Mind map type 2: Display mind mapping

This mind map is used to communicate the practice of a specific concept to your audience. Demo mindmaps illustrate how the job works and allow you to track the progress. A demonstration mind map's audience is what will attract your attention, and not the topic. The viewers ability to comprehend the information is key in determining where the information should be located on the map. If your audience can follow what you are displaying, the map will be nicely organized. Your demonstration can then be accepted by viewers.

This type of thoughtmap is used for presenting a development in ideas. These thoughts maps help you monitor and visualize the various measures, as well as the information associated with each one. The demonstration mindmap, in contrast to the one that is used for reference, is more focused on the dialogue and helps to envision the flow of the conversation, as opposed to repressing it through the accumulations of thoughts. This approach focuses on the attendees and not the topic. Although the brain map is based on the primary issue, the discussion with the group will control it.

This type of mindmap can be used for the following:

It is possible to map specific consumer behavior using a solution. You can also include the steps the customer took to help you track a specific target like buying a product, or subscribing your site.

Trainees should stick to a consistent stream of information even in training sessions. It is a simplified PowerPoint presentation with a clearer strategy.

Discuss a scenario and the actions that can be taken to resolve it.

This type can be used to help you describe an action, or a coaching session. Here are some examples. Sunday activities mind map

#mindmap 3: Tunnel timeline and mind maps

This kind of mindmap will also be simplified by planning brain channel. They are used primarily to create a job plan, a program plan, or for problem solving. Tunnel thought maps are used to reach a goal. This type of mindmap is used to visualize success. The center (main subject) of this mind map represents the outcome you wish to pursue. Each subtopic represents a pathway to that goal. It's possible to follow the roadmap to achieve success.

Preparing for a job, or choosing activities from other activities, can be done with the preparation map. This mind map will show the different activities and possible connections between them. This type of mindmap may be used for job plans, action programs, problem solving, and other similar programs. This brainmap's core subject reflects the desired end result. Each sub-topic is meant to help you reach your core goal. For example, a core idea may be to increase the market share x percent. A sub-topic could focus on the strategies to accomplish this goal. These types of thought maps might be used to reach next.

Plan jobs and build a job program that can be achieved through specific actions.

To solve problems, place the search for an answer at the forefront of your mind and discuss the potential solutions with the group during the following session.

This type of mind map could be used to solve problems or plan for job planning. These are just a few examples: mind map of marketing plan.

Mind maps can be powerful tools for brainstorming ideas, creating project plans, and solving problems. The three types mentioned earlier can cover virtually every type of mind map. The functions and characteristics of each type can help you achieve the results you desire with brain mapping.

A headmap can be a powerful tool to generate creative ideas, plan strategies and solve problems. Incorrect implementation of the procedure can lead to many mind mapping sessions being neglected. Facilitators must choose the most effective mindmap for the meeting to ensure a flourishing mind-mapping group. The three above brain maps cover most of the functions brain maps can be used. For the brain map session to produce the desired results, it is crucial to know the features of each type and how they can be used.

Types of mindmaps

Mind mapping is a technique that allows for nonlinear analysis and development of solutions. Use felt tip pen on flip-chart paper, markers on whiteboards, or pc-mind-mapping computer software to produce mind-maps. Mind maps can contain phrases, linking links, lines, and sometimes drawings. Head maps are useful for project understanding and problem solving.

#problem-fixing maps

It is a great tool for brainstorming with staff members. The goal is to think quickly, and not have to go through logical reviews. It is possible for team members and others to see the brain map throughout the semester. This allows them to generate more ideas. This gives rise to positive momentum and helps solve problems.

The leader starts a brainstorming session by writing down the issue. The recorder brings colored spokes radiating out of the heart issue, as staff members interact with one another. Each spoke can be used to represent a different area of the matter. Staff comments are used to add smaller lines and arrows between different objects.

The brainstorming session should be the only time that problem-solving minds maps are used. Members of the team will share their thoughts and ideas with each other, then they can create the map, assign priorities, and set action items. This is made easier by the brainmap. Mind maps typically last only a few minutes.

#projectmaps

The project thought maps can be useful for planning events, item launches, closing massive sales, and many other activities. They are kept current to reflect any changes in job status and they last only until the job is complete. Job mind maps typically last for only a few weeks or months.

#knowledge maps

Knowledge mind maps allow you to store information once it is done and keep it safe for future use. Some can be refined and updated over time, while others cannot. Mind maps can help you understand mind maps. When used on multiple occasions over a long time, understanding mindmaps is crucial in keeping corporate background, the knowledge that was never recorded and which exists only within the heads of workers. In order to help new workers discover old procedures for performing repetitive actions, knowledge mindmaps may be extremely valuable. The lifespan of mind maps that are understood can be many years.

How mindmaps can be used to help creative thinking

A mindmap is a visual tool that allows teams to store and organize their ideas. Mind maps help teams solve problems naturally by allowing them to group subtopics together in an ordered fashion.

Thoughts maps, which are not difficult to review or misaligned meetings, bring together teams and make it easier to collaborate on a variety of jobs.

5 types mind maps

There are five types. There are five types of head maps: straightforward, concept, and random word thought maps. These can be used to encourage freeform brainstorming among any group. Agile teams use flowcharts for preparation and planning.

1. Simple mind map

Mind maps are visual diagrams that look like a shrub or tree. They show important groups radiating from one central node. Lower categories represent the sub-branches for larger ones.

A mindmap in miro is a free default app. It is possible for you to concentrate on your true thoughts, and only a few hotkeys are required to create the map. Miro makes it possible to include images, videos, and other visuals in your brainmap. This will encourage you and help expand your thinking.

These are the steps to making your map.

Start by looking at a blank canvas. Give your mind permission to express and share ideas naturally and freely.

You can include colours in your brain map.

Online, you can only use one keyword. This gives your brain map more power and flexibility.

Take pictures everywhere. A photo is worth a million terms and can be used to inspire others.

2. Concept map

A concept map shows how theories are connected in a brainstorming session. An idea is an idea frame. It is defined by a clear "focus question". A mapped theory is a hierarchical structure that helps you understand the issue more clearly and builds stronger arguments.

The brain map of a concept map is distinct from its design. It usually follows a hierarchical layout and reveals more complicated interrelations of theories (a theory could relate to more that one mother node).

To map your theories, all you need is to pay attention to the ideas. This is an easy guide for the process:

Insert a sticker or form with the overall topic you wish more information about. Ensure that the answer is specific.

Brainstorm a list of topics that relate to the topic. Sticky notes are bulk-add and can be used to guide your thought process.

Next, create a map of topics around the idea. Connect them by lines. It is best to place the most important ideas near the border. The less significant ideas should stay closer to it. Use text to better describe the connections.

3. Random words

Random phrases is a brainstorming technique. It stimulates creativity and encourages you to find new perspectives. It's possible to find fresh solutions by looking around.

To find the solution to the problem you need, force yourself to use a random term. This is how you can make use of this brainstorming method.

Identify the problem you are facing.

Make an initial node using a Mind Map tool. Use random notes as the note. This term should be completely arbitrary, and not relevant to your issue.

Make sure to use shortcuts when writing down ideas that are related or connected to an arbitrary word.

You can use a remark device to look at the connections between your arbitrary organizations and your difficulty. Write down all the thoughts you have.

4. Flowchart

A flowchart depicts an incremental workflow or process and is illustrated with contours that are different from others, as well as arranged with arrows.

Flowcharts can be used to illustrate a specific process in order help identify, understand and eliminate bottlenecks. There are many types to flowcharts. Although some flowcharts need particular shapes (such ovals and diamonds), most will work with text boxes.

The best way of creating a flowchart is:

You can start thinking by including the original product.

To begin to make a connection with your mind mapping apps, use the control dots surrounding the first thing. It will be easy to navigate the menu and choose the next option, allowing you to create your thought flow as quickly as possible.

You can personalize the appearance and feel by adding item menus to both arrows, and objects to this flowchart.

5. Dialogue map

Dialogue mapping allows for facilitation. This facilitates a shared understanding of the wicked problem.

It is common for a group or individuals to gather together to resolve a complex or challenging problem. But how do they see it all and what is the real issue? Teams around the world can view the big picture in realtime. They can share shared knowledge, remote access and knowledge retention. The built in brain mapping tool will help you dig deeper and create a better solution.

Dialogue mapping contrasts nicely to agile practices. It may be an extremely effective instrument to provide clarity, focus and advice about agile actions. You could even use it to have retrospective meetings. It will help you understand what improvement is needed by the agile groups. You can make a dialogmap by following these steps:

Create the first node with all the mind mapping tools. Start with a query. You could start with "agenda?" It might be as simple or as complicated, as in "agenda?"

Add thoughts to your mind using shortcuts For every idea, you can add "pro", "con" and "neutral" arguments. Use the brain map bar to highlight positives or drawbacks.

For mutual understanding, compile a list listing all of the items you have identified.

Head maps: paper vs virtual

Mind maps are fast replacing summaries, lists, summary, and other linear forms of business for a variety applications. Use mind maps in work, college, and other mundane applications such as grocery store and to-do list management, can be beneficial for almost anyone.

They were performed traditionally using paper and pencil.

This is a great way to create mind maps that can be used at any time and anywhere you want. This method may be used even by people who are not familiar with technology.

Sometimes, handwriting helps with learning. You can add as many colour and as many examples to your map as desired.

Unfortunately, hand-drawn ones can not be considered the best.

They could also get dirty, lose their way, or tear apart. They take longer to make than a virtual one. Virtual ones can also be created with mind mapping tools, of which many are available, and have some advantages over handdrawn.

They are quicker to make, easier to modify, cost-effective, and require no space. Plus, they look professional.

Virtual maps do have their disadvantages. For example, you need a computer in order to create them. Sometimes people find that they want to make a map at home and then use it at work.

These issues can, however, be solved by a fantastic mind mapping program.

This allows for you to create an account on any pc. That's a tremendous benefit if it's work-related work on your home or work pcs.

It is possible to save maps created at work so that you can continue to work from home. It lets you create a mental map in your home, on your computer, while on a long trip, or bus ride, and then take it to work to share with coworkers.

While traditional pen-and–paper methods are equally effective for virtual tasks, such as increasing business and productivity, many people are now discovering that digital maps can be easier to store and share. It is possible to make modifications to virtual mindmaps without making them messy like newspaper.

You can make brainstorm maps with all the software you need. This is why they are rapidly becoming a favorite of people from all walks.

Chapter 4: What Is Mind Mapping Anyway?

A mindmap revolves around a single idea or concept. An image is placed at the center of the page. Associative ideas can then be added such as words or portions of words or images. When creating a mindmap, it is important to link the major ideas to one central concept. The ideas that follow can be expanded on from them. A mind map can be either a simple or complex diagram, depending on how fast you are, for example, during a lecture. Mind mapping is a highly effective method to transfer information from your brain to other areas. This creative method allows you to take and write notes that help map your ideas. All mind maps have one common feature. They are structured in a way that expands from the center. And they use simple concepts like images, lines, colors, symbols and words. Mind mapping has the advantage of converting monotonous information into a memorable, colorful, well-organized image that is compatible for your brain's natural way of working. A city map is a simple way to grasp the concept of mind-mapping. The city center represents the core idea. The main roads running from the city centre represent the key thought, and the branches or subsidiary roads represent your secondary ideas. Images and shapes with special meanings can indicate particular ideas, landmarks or interests.

We now know what mind mapping looks like. Let us now look at the benefits.

Mind Mapping is used for various purposes

It is important that you fully understand mind mapping, its benefits and how you can use them in your daily lives. It is often used by writers to help them organize their thoughts. Here are some examples of mind mapping applications:

Taking meeting notes

A mind map can be a great way for you to record the ideas that were discussed in a meeting. Meetings are not linear and rarely follow a fixed agenda. They usually involve a lot of discussion, information sharing, and ideas. Text notes are technical linear and make it difficult to capture ideas in meetings efficiently, especially if they are nonlinear.

Book Summaries

Mind maps are particularly effective for book summaries. There are many ideas and concepts in books, even nonfiction ones that you must capture. If you love to read and often take notes along the way, it's possible you have felt the need add another concept or idea to a particular idea on another paper. Perhaps you wanted to look at older notes to help make connections. This can be a challenge if you are using text. It may also lead to disorganized notes. Mind maps are great tools for summarizing information. It is possible to create branches that represent key concepts and ideas. Then, organize your notes so you are able to easily understand them.

Project Management

While there are many software and tools to help manage projects, you can also use mind maps to manage smaller projects. To start, your core idea can be represented as the main work project. Next, the following branches can be created:

*Budget
*People
*Deadline
*Resources
*Scope

These branches are the heart of any project. This allows you to easily create a mindmap with them in order to manage the project. As you move forward with the project, you will be able to review your branches regularly after you've set them up.

Studying

Mind maps can prove to be extremely useful, especially for students. It's possible to use them to take notes and connect the dots in preparation for exams and tests. If you already have a mental picture of what you are trying to remember, you can use the mindmap to quickly connect the dots and understand the material. As such, the mind map will help you understand the main idea without you needing to remember the details. Once you have a good grasp of the key concepts and strokes you will be able easily to apply them (with practice) and solve your problems like a pro.

Goal Setting

Every person has a goal in life. As most people, your goal setting process is a tedious one. This isn't a bad idea. This method has been successful for many people for centuries. However, mind maps can be a much more effective method of setting goals. It is easy to remember your goals when you use mind mapping. Why? They use visualization. By drawing your goals on a sheet of paper, you can visualise the final results. Your goals can be visualized on a page. This will help you to implement them.

Problem-Solving

There are many methods for solving problems. However, the 5W+1H outline is an excellent way to get started. It asks you

several questions that you need to answer.
*Who
*Where
*How
*What
*When
This is a great example of mind mapping because it lets you explore each section in detail and allows you to find connections between your answers. These relationships are easy to spot on a map. As you begin to answer all these questions, your problem will become clearer. The solution will then become more obvious. To use mind mapping to solve your problem, make your main idea your main idea. The branches represent the questions. This will help you to find solutions to your problems.

Brainstorming

There are many ideas that can be generated from brainstorming. Sometimes, not all of them make sense. It's easy to organize all your ideas into a mindmap. Then, later, you can use them to make sensible decisions. This is what we will discuss later.

Knowledge Management

A lot of people rely upon taking notes on paper and reading the text to learn a specific topic. This can sometimes prove inefficient, especially when trying to recall information from many pages. It would be awkward and cumbersome for you to reread all these notes. However, you can easily create a mind map to help you find the most relevant ideas. Instead of writing notes to collect information, mind mapping can be used to add knowledge to your library. Knowledge management can be easy and effective with software-based mindmaps. You can create a knowledge base on business networking by taking this example. There are many PDF files that include tips and text notes on great business networking books. What is the best way of creating a knowledgebank using all this information in different formats? The key is to make all this information central and tie it all together. A single mindmap can help you organize all the information. It will also serve as your knowledgebank. You can organize this information with branches in mindmaps. They are easy to use and will make it simple to access.

Doing Things Right

Mind maps can be helpful in representing information in an easily understood format. But they're not as useful when it comes time to create a to do list. That is where pen and note will be more useful. It doesn't necessarily mean you should not use mind mapping to get things done. Mind maps can be very helpful, especially when you use productivity techniques such as agile results.

Decision-Making

You can always have a wide range of options when you face a situation that calls for a decision. Pen and paper, or mind maps, can be helpful. All of these methods involve writing out options, but mind maps can make the options visually for easy follow-up. This is important, especially when you are considering different options. It's easy to make associations between different options due to its visual nature. This is especially true when you map the scenarios. When you do this, it is much easier to connect multiple options to determine the best.

The next chapters will cover the specific ways mind mapping can be used in different areas. Before we get on to the specifics, let's look at some of the mind mapping tools that you can use.

Why Mind Mapping

Because the mind leaps between one thing and another, and not necessarily in an ordered manner, linear thinking can prove to be extremely restricting. Mind mapping helps to avoid linear thought processes. Mind mapping can open up new ways of thinking and allow you to be more creative. Some might say that mind maps are more realistic and useful than lists. This is because they, like almost all of life are not well-organized or ridged.

Mind mapping stimulates problem-solving because you can tap into your right brain area, where creativity, intuition, and creativity can be helpful. Not all problems and challenges can be arranged in an outline.

Let's pretend you have ten important things to do today. To make sure you don't forget what you need to do tonight, take out a slip or lined paper. This is your finished list.

Do Today!
*Gase up truck
*Lunch at Tony
*Email manager.
*Grocery for birthday party foods.
*Finish PowerPoint presentation to be delivered on Thursday
*Gym--spinning class.
*Pay bills online now
*Support Susie with the science projects.
*Call client to set up next meeting.
*Give Spot your bath.

You record your items in a linear format with a plain, numerical layout. It is basically a list of everything you have to do today. There aren't any images, colors, or other visuals to create a visually stimulating and interesting list.

You can use the mind mapping technique to create a "To-Do Today" checklist in a sprawling layout with more space between each item. Each item should be separated into work and personal (or professional and personal, depending on what you prefer). In order to engage your right brain, color and connector lines are a great way to add color to text.

To-Do Today-style mind mapping lists could have pictures and color to make the list more memorable. For example, the task "Give Spot some bath" could be illustrated with a drawing showing Spot sitting next to a tub. The mind map's qualities are richer and more vivid, and the colors enhance each component.

A to-do/list is a way to keep track of the tasks you have to do in a set time, in this example, for a single working day. There are several reasons why a written to-do list is problematic. First, it is not easy to memorize. Second, you must review the list many times throughout the day. It can be time-consuming, and it can be frustrating, to hunt for the list. It is impossible to refer to the list if you lose it. Additionally, the list was not designed to be stored in your memory so you might forget many items.

Mind mapping allows you the ability to create your "To Do Today" list and still use a checkmark system. This can give many people a sense of accomplishment. You can place small boxes beside each line item to help you check off completed tasks.

Building Mind Maps The Right Way

Though brainstorming and mind-mapping are not the exact same, they can be used in combination to achieve common goals.

Mind mapping is not just about brainstorming, but also involves thinking, planning, and taking notes. You can also use many office products for brainstorming, including Flip-charts (3x5 index cards), Post-it Notes, Flip-Charts, flip-charts, and Mind Maps (3x5 Index Cards).

Brainstorming--it's intended to expand your thoughts on a certain topic or subject. This is done often in groups, meetings, and as part a team.

Mind mapping - This can then be used for organizing the brainstorming session results and revealing the relationships between ideas.

There are two stages to the two-stage process. Stage 1 is about free thinking. Stage 2 is about organizing. For the best results, it is important to complete these stages in the correct order.

Stage One

Brainstorming = Free Thinking + Procreating Ideas

Place your problem or topic on a white piece of paper.

For free association, use colored pencils or markers. Any topic or subject that interests you, write it down and draw on the piece. You should not edit the paper or make any changes to it. Instead, let your thoughts and ideas run wild, no matter how crazy or ridiculous they might seem.

Stage 2

Mind Mapping = Identifying Relationships + Organising Ideas

Create a mindmap by connecting the dots between the key ideas and points of your brainstorming paper using words, lines and arrows.

After you have completed step 2, you can now look at your mindmap and identify similarities and contrasts.

Mind Mapping, The Analogy Method

Analogy refers to the process of shifting ideas, concepts or thoughts from another area to find a solution.

1. You will need to create two branches on a sheet of paper. Label one "Ideas", the other "Concept Area".

2. The Concept Area can be expanded to include a sub-branch that provides more space for subjects you are proficient in. The topics could include "knottying", "toy-shipbuilding", or "accounting." They don't need to be related or relevant to the problem you are solving.

3. You should list the major concepts for each of these topics in step 2. You could use "figure 8, "overhand knot", "double fisherman's knot," "Strangle knot" to describe the knot-tying area.

4. Now you can move your ideas from step 3. You can use some of the knot-tying books to find creative solutions to problems such as creating costumes for plays. You might find the solution in "Overhand knot", if one set needed to be changed on-stage from a suit for a man to a long skirt for a women.

Chapter 5: Mind Mapping Tips And Strategies

There are many helpful tips, as well as the information you will find in this book. These were also created by people like yourself. People who were interested in organizing their lives through this process and decided to experiment with it.

We hope to take some trial out of the process so you can jump right into using it to its fullest potential.

Along the way, you will discover your own tips & tricks. We hope that you will be able to share your discoveries with others who are just beginning this journey.

Tips for Mind Mapping Success

Your first draft doesn't need to be the final. Just as with all other things, you can create many versions until the layout you like. The final product is what's most important.

Make sure to mind map where you are the most relaxed. Enjoy music, or simply sit in your preferred spot. Let the ideas flow.

If you are drawing a map of creativity, you can trace the outline and then change your colors. This will give you freedom to alter your ideas as needed.

Make a daily template of the map that you can use for your daily navigation needs.

Keep your mindmaps close by. You can keep them in your organizer or email them to yourself. It doesn't matter what, having them around the day will help you keep on track to completing a task or achieving a goal.

It is important to not take time to think when you are writing. This can seem counterproductive. But the point is to give yourself permission to let your ideas flow naturally. After you have finished your first draft, you will be able to go back and examine the details.

Make sure you leave enough room. You may want to add more information, or you can assume that you will, if you create a mindmap. Space is always more important than time.

Your agenda does not need to be in a certain order. Focus on what you are putting in the information. Mind mapping allows you to connect the dots later.

Accelerating Mind mapping

Mind mapping is an effective way to organize thoughts and ideas. Professionals who use it as a tool for organizing their thoughts and ideas often seek out ways to speed things up so that they can do it quickly and efficiently.

There are many options to speed up mind mapping, depending on your needs.

It is possible to make it faster and more enjoyable.

a)Use One Color

Black and white can help you achieve your Mind mapping goals, even though it is an important tool in the Mind mapping strategy.

Saving time is a big benefit.

Additionally, it will help you save time as you are not required to stop and think about color choices and how they can be used to express your ideas.

While color is a fun way to create exciting mind maps, it can also help you to recognize ideas with different levels and to group them together. However, leaving out the color can make you save some time that you don't need to spend.

You can always go back and color the branches after you have reviewed and organized the content.

You can integrate color with ease by using a highlighter or colored crayon. These highlighters are great for highlighting key information and distinguishing it from other ideas and thoughts.

b. Paintbrush Pens and Markers

Color can be used to connect and separate ideas in your Mind Map. There are ways you can include it while still speeding up the process.

Use of colored pencils and markers can take longer as you must color in the branches, image or doodles contained on your Map.

The process is much quicker and easier if you use a marker or pen that has a paintbrush tip.

Most people create mindmaps with branches that change from thicker and thinner like branches on trees.

You'll need to spend considerable time coloring in the lines with a fine-tip marker or pen to achieve this effect.

A paintbrush pen or marker is a great tool to help create that thick to slender look in just a few strokes

c. Quick and simple images and drawings

While beautifully designed mindmaps are amazing and fun to do, don't waste time by drawing perfect images.

Although it may be time-consuming and fun to create an intricate, beautiful central image, with lots of details and color, it can also be creatively satisfying. You may also find it a time-consuming chore if you are trying to meet a tight deadline. The quality of the artwork you create isn't as important than the memory it creates inside your head. Remember why mind mapping is important. This is not for the sake of getting into fine arts programs. Let your mind wander and let your drawing flow. Stick figures will suffice.

d. Do not mind mapping everything

Mind mapping is a useful strategy for creating complex ideas, comparing them, and organizing complicated thoughts.

It works best when it is used to help you understand and develop complex ideas.

With this in view, Mind maps won't be able to capture all the information you need to remember. In such cases, you can opt for linear note-taking and flashcards.

Some information is not relevant to the mind-mapping strategies discussed above. Not all the information you need to remember or learn is required to be mind mapped. Here's an example of someone who overmapped (for want of a better word).

It is a better deal.

It has lost all its utility as a tool. It is difficult to comprehend and far too overwhelming.

While you read, brainstorm ideas and come up with new ideas, take a moment to think about what you really need to organize.

If you don't feel certain aspects of the information that you are reviewing or creating are relevant, don't bother mapping it.

e. Use A3-Sized paper

You can mind map any topic with A3 paper. It provides the best orient to radiant thinking.

If you use A4-sized paper, it may be that you find yourself needing to constantly create new mindmaps because you don't have enough space for all of your information on one page.

A3 paper is convenient in size and orientation. To keep your mind maps organized and easily accessible, you can buy an A3-sized art notebook.

This will reduce the number and complexity of your central images. It also means that your mindmaps won't be spread across multiple pages. Your mind maps become easier to complete and much more enjoyable to use when they are done.

f. A Daily Basis Mind Map

Just as with any skill you are working on, the more that you practice mind mapping the quicker it will become second nature and the more impressive your results.

It is also a good idea to practice Mind mapping and refine your skills so that you can find a method that fits your needs professionally and personally.

It is common for people who are unfamiliar with the concept of mind mapping to have difficulty creating them quickly.

The tendency of newbies to restrict or hinder the natural flow and thought process is to ask questions such as, "Am I doing this correctly?" or"Do my pictures look silly?

Many people, especially those who are just starting to master mind mapping, may find themselves having to discard their maps and re-create them multiple times before they complete the final piece.

This is counterproductive to the purpose for the mapping process.

However, with some practice, you'll be able to create your own unique techniques that suit your professional and personal needs.

g. Make this a daily routine

It is easy not to remember to do the mind mapping steps outlined above. To help you remember to use your mind mapping process more often, it is a simple trick to make sure you have all the items that you need at hand.

Consider leaving your pen, paper, and book on the surface where you work, like the coffee table, your desk or the kitchen table.

These items will serve as reminders to Mind-map every spare moment. Mind mapping only takes 15 minutes per day. This is enough time for you to get a few important ideas covered and to help you improve your Mind-mapping skills. Mind mapping is so useful and productive, but it's easy to forget how to put it in practice.

It will all become second nature to you! We are confident that you will reap the rewards of the process far more than any possible frustration.

Chapter 6: How The Human Brain Learns

The human mind cannot learn by being forced to memorize or learning from familiar situations. Instead, it gets lazy and forgets. The brain can learn from new stimuli that make it more effective in memory and learning, such as images. Images reach the right-hemisphere and promote creativity.

The brain is not made up of individual areas that can function independently, but rather a network of interconnected areas known as hemispheres. Emotions are crucial in learning. They reach the amygdala. It is the same with tastes, sounds, images and smells. So, stories that are meaningful to us, that move and touch us, will always be recorded. Mind Maps use images or photos that evoke such emotions that they will remain with us forever.

The stimulation of the brain comes from interaction between people. People working together in a collaborative and cooperative fashion stimulates their brains, which increases motivation, creativity and attention. This is a side that helps us to better understand concepts and ideas. Mind Maps permit such collaboration, with each member of the working group contributing ideas.

Linear and lateral thinking

Mind Mapping is a system where ideas and concepts can be connected to each other like the brain's neural networks. The brain uses both hemispheres together to learn and understand better.

This method of learning is more effective as it incorporates the talents of both hemispheres. The left hemisphere is the rational and analytical, where logic is found, and the right is home to creativity, intuition, artistic, and musical skills, among many other things.

There are times and problems that require logical reasoning, linear thinking and logic. The left hemisphere can respond to those needs. Other problems require imagination, creativity and lateral think, which are all available in the right-hemisphere. Mind Maps stimulate this right half.

Mind Maps encourage creativity and lateral thinking. Mind Mapping encourages creativity.

Mind Maps, Concept Maps

Both tools can be used to learn ideas and concepts visually. Everything will be different once that point is made. There are many things that can be done to make your concept maps different.

Mind Mapping example for Global Warming

Concept Mapping Example - Climate Change

27 ONLINE SOLUTIONS

Tony Buzan prefers to draw Mind Maps by hand. But, because it's important to be creative in order for you to generate practical ideas and think creatively, technology tools can also prove useful, especially if the exhibition or presentation is on-line.

Because of new technologies, Mind Maps can be created with many tools. This makes it easy to find the one that you like or the best.

Next you will find a link list that allows you to create Mind Maps which are visually appealing and very useful. They are ordered alphabetically, and not according to importance. This is because it depends on individual tastes and needs.

* Ayoa formerly iMindMap

Tony Buzan is the creator of Mind Maps Online. This online tool is unique in that it has his approval. App that allows users to create and customize Mind Maps. It promotes creativity, brainstorming as well as non-linear reasoning.

A freemium software with limited content. The cost for the paid version of the app is EUR 10 per head. You can download an offline application that's compatible with Windows OS or Mac OS.

It can be shared to all members of a work group or educational group. Everyone can access and modify it at anytime. The ability to attach images and notes as well as audio files is another great benefit.

* Bubbl.us

Software that allows you create concept and mind maps without needing to install or run any applications. Many colors, shapes and designs available to personalize your Mind Maps.

It can also be downloaded as an Image and shared with students, colleagues, and coworkers. Multi-device Tool: You can use it on your smartphone, tablet, and computer.

* Coggle

Online software to create and share Mind Maps.

It is easy to use. It allows for images, links and share folders. You also get notifications via email.

It is a freemium software that allows you make as many Mind Maps (up to one) as you like, though all of them are public. The paid version costs $ 5 per monthly and allows you to keep the maps private.

* CMap Tools

Simple tool for developing concept maps. It is completely free, and you can share the maps you create with other people to help them realize their ideas.

It can also be downloaded for any operating system like Windows, Mac OS, or Linux.

* ConceptDraw

Software that supports a wide range of images and links. This software allows collaboration between members in a group and can be used to add to Power Point presentations.

* Creately

This freemium program allows you to create as many as five Mind Maps. Great Mind Maps can either be created online or downloaded the app. The interface is simple to use, and it allows you to quickly create them. This also allows for collaboration between colleagues or students.

* EDraw Mindmap

This tool does not offer a web version. Instead, you can use it only from the downloaded application. It can either be used from a computer or on a mobile device. It includes ready-made templates that can be used as a basis if the user does not know the basics of the tool. There are also many other tools, such backgrounds, objects symboles, etc.

It can even be exported. Ease in inclusion in Power Point presentations.

It offers discounted prices to individuals, schools and companies.

* Gliffy

Paid application with its associated free trial. If the user decides that they want to purchase the software, the cost per month is $ 5. Group application that allows members to collaborate simultaneously and receive updates instantly.

* GoConqr

An online tool that is free to download and can be used from a smartphone or tablet. Mind Maps are also available to share with colleagues and to be printed. For greater versatility, you can attach images.

A simple-to-use interface allows you to quickly create Mind Maps and get great results.

* iMindQ

This online application can easily be accessed from a computer via its website.

Like the other ones, files can be attached, as well as notes or links. A unique feature is that it integrates with Dropbox so users can save and store Mind Maps.

* Mapul

This tool allows you and your collaborators to create mind maps using a web-based application.

The freemium version has a limited functionality and can be used to create Mind Maps, export as jpg, or create presentations. But, with the paid version starting at $ 25, per quarter, it is possible to create unlimited Mind Maps.

* MindGenius

This tool is limited to a 14-day complimentary trial. It has higher payment plans than other tools because it has access not only to Mind Maps but also other types.

It's only available for Windows 7 operating systems. This tool is very user-friendly and easy to use.

* MindManager

You have the option of getting it for free for 30 days without having your credit card registered. The paid version is available for Windows and Mac OS OS operating systems, but it costs over $ 400.

It is an affordable tool that is widely used, even though it has a high price. Mind Maps, however, can be created in beautiful ways. There are also other tools that focus more on the business world and less on the educational.

It allows the sharing of content with clients and colleagues on any device as well as exporting it to more than 700 websites.

* MindMapFree

You can quickly create a Mind Map by using this free tool. Ideal for individuals who don't need to develop complex and complicated solutions.

* MindMaple

Online tool. There is a free, but limited, version as well as a paid version that includes many more features. It supports touch screen electronic pen. The tool is compatible with Windows, Mac OS, iOS and Android operating systems ($5 to $10).

It allows the creation of Mind Maps with notes, links, and files. You can also export them in Word, Excel, Power Point or other formats.

* MindMeister

This is one the most well-known softwares. It has been used by more than 7,000,000 people. It is available in two formats: from the app or in web format. However, it is not recommended as the web version can be quite powerful.

It is available for free (limited to 3 Mind Maps), and with a paid edition starting from EUR 5. It can be used with Windows,

Mac OS, Linux or Mac OS operating systems.

The program offers many functions such as different styles, designs, and the ability attach links and multi-media files, and to export them into a presentation.

Mind Maps can be generated, but you can also plan projects and hold brainstorming sessions. It allows you work on a Mind Map and sharing it with your fellow members.

* MindMup

The paid version is quite expensive but you can make great mind maps with it. It allows you quickly to make unlimited Mind Maps. The program allows you to create unlimited Mind Maps quickly by exporting them in Power Point, PDF, or Power Point.

* MindNode

One of the most useful and widely-used tools for Apple environments. This tool is available for Mac OS and iOS. It allows unlimited mind maps to be created. There are many styles and designs available. Images can be attached and exported in either open format, text or images. They can then be stored in iCloud. It has a simple, intuitive interface.

* Mindomo

Online tool that is only in Italian. We can open it with Chrome browser and use the translator option at bottom of the web address. It can be accessed via the website or downloaded for use on mobile devices.

Free version: Up to 3 Mind Maps can be created and shared. For EUR 5.5, the price includes more options like exporting Mind Maps into different formats or importing multimedia files.

* Mind Vector

It is an online tool for creating Mind Maps. The interface is simple. It is available in both a web-based format and as an app for mobile devices that run on Android or iOS. Although it has a limited number of features (limited to 3 Mind Maps), the paid version ($9.99) offers unlimited access to all the tools.

Mind Maps may be saved to your Cloud so they can always be accessed and accessed by an unlimited amount of collaborators. This allows attachments of files such as images and notes as well as exporting Mind Maps into different formats.

* MindView

Mind Map Maker is a professional tool that allows you create Mind Maps. This tool supports many types of templates, diagrams, and other functionalities.

The 30-day free trial is included with the paid version. Monthly subscriptions start at $ 15.

* Popplet

Application available only in web format (free), iPad (paid).

Its interface is very simple, and it makes it easy for you to quickly start creating Mind Maps.

* Simplemind

Online Mind Mapping tool. Available for Mac OS, Windows, and mobile devices (iOS/Android) in English. Although the free version has limited features, it can be used for a short time. For full access to all features, you need to upgrade to the paid version that starts at $ 9.99 mobile devices.

Images, photos icons, links and icons can all be imported. Mind Maps are also possible to export in PDF or image format. They can also stored using cloud solutions like Dropbox and Google Drive.

* SpiderScribe

Online tool that allows you to create Mind Maps in a limited way. You can also make 3 of your own Mind Maps.

Tool that is focused on Mind Maps & Brainstorming. Its main feature is sharing Mind Maps easily with other collaborators/workgroup colleagues. Mind Maps are stored in the cloud and can be accessed from anywhere, on any device.

* The Brain

This free tool can either be downloaded to the computer's desk and used from there or online.

* WiseMapping

Mind Map creator software that can be used online to create Mind Maps. You can share Mind Maps online and even insert them into webpages. A simple interface, with many functionalities, allows you to import images and link, and export Mind Maps.

* XMind

Software with both a free and a paid version. Starting at $ 39.99 / 6 Months with all the functionality. The free version can be used to create Mind Maps and share them among your coworkers. Available for Mac OS X, Windows and Linux as well mobile devices.

It allows for the import of images, notes and links as well as exporting Mind Maps as Office environment formats or in PDF. The Mind Maps can also be synced with Evernote. It is the most widely used tool. You can also make unlimited Mind Maps using the free version. This is due to its excellent design that includes numerous functionalities, image bank templates and templates. You can save them in your cloud (XMind Cloud), so that they're available to everyone in the group.

Chapter 7: Education Made Easier With Mind Mapping

Mind Mapping Tools are loved for their versatility.

They can be used both for personal and business reasons, as well as for educational purposes.

These tools combine different techniques and strategies to make learning for students easier.

Mind mapping is an essential tool for students. It allows them to arrange educational topics in a logical way.

It was determined that visual effects have a greater impact than traditional instruments. Thus, visual aids should be used to enhance learning.

They are useful because they allow images and maps to be used as educational mapping tools. Mind mapping is a great way to learn by using images, charts, diagrams and other visuals.

Teachers and students are able to use this tool to help them organize information about a topic. You can place an object on a page using mind mapping tools. All related ideas, thoughts and ideas surround it.

Mind mapping techniques are useful in secure transmitting large amounts of information.

Teachers can organize their lectures quickly and easily for their students.

This tool is simple and easy to use. It can be used every day.

Students, on the contrary, can organise and present their information clearly. You can create better notes and texts than you can with traditional methods.

A map of a subject or topic can cover all aspects of it.

This allows for the main ideas to be digested quickly, and also makes it easier to understand long theories.

Students can structure the subject in such a way that they understand it better and make learning easier. You can also link related topics to the main theme or concept.

Education is a complex field that requires lots of information and data. Therefore, you will need a helpful tool.

Mind mapping is a great tool for any task in the education environment.

Mind mapping makes it possible to make revolutionary changes in learning and teaching practices at college, university, and kindergarten levels.

It's simple to learn and remember logically ordered, well-managed and organized information with the use of mental mapping software.

Learning is about discovering new things. Teachers and instructors use many techniques to facilitate and facilitate education.

Mind mapping is another popular tool. People use this to optimize their abilities. You can manage your thoughts and work faster.

It is possible to use mapping techniques in order to achieve good results in all areas of life, not just education.

It also provides an example of the practical applications for educational mind mapping.

Creative Thinking Exercises: Mind Mapping Mind Mapping in Creative Thinking Exercises

To improve your creativity there are some things you should know.

According to psychological research they include colour, shape and unique features.

Research shows that mindmaps are one of the best tools to promote creativity. It promotes creativity, flexibility, and innovation.

What are the representations in the mind? Mind Maps consist of lines and bubbles representing concepts and relationships.

The central theme is located at the center of related topics. The central theme is then divided into several related topics.

It is possible to use mind mapping as an artistic tool to help you generate many innovative and creative ideas.

There are five stages to creative thinking.
1) The Quickfire

Mind Map Burst Pick any topic. Draw a central photo on a piece or content of paper to represent the theme. It will help to let ideas flow as quickly and easily as possible in order to foster new ideas.

You may find certain ideas unlogical or meaningless at first. However, you can write them down later if they prove to be helpful.

2) Next Rewrite & Restoration

Take a quick break. Relax and think. Make another but make sure to classify any tentative dreams. You can make hierarchies. Be aware that you should pay attention to similar ideas. Mind maps enable individuals to explore and develop their thoughts.

3) Incubation

Your brain can think creatively when it is not stressed (sleeping and daydreaming, running etc.). This stage can be a breakthrough for many people.

4) Second Reconstruction And Revision

Your current view of the first and second mindmaps is at this stage. You can now create a different one. Take the data from Steps 1 and 2 to create a final planning.

5) Final Stage

Once you've created your final mindmap, you just need to start looking for solutions, accomplishments, and decisions.

You'll be amazed by how creative and innovative your ideas are once you've gone through the five stages.

Mind mapping software can be downloaded for those not familiar with the subject.

Computer-based brain mapping is just as effective as traditional spiritual mapping.

Mind mapping can be used to uncover your creative thoughts.

Mind Maps for Optimizing Your Thinking

Mind Maps can help you optimize your thinking

You finally decided to take the long-awaited vacation you had been waiting for.

You're traveling in open roads where you've never been before. What do you want to do first? OK, now that you have claimed you are mum, you can look at the map. Most people do. Except if they're spontaneous or if you travel in space.

We can use maps not only to find our way to home but also to automate our trips. We can use navigation websites or programs to locate the fastest route, save gas and avoid traffic.

We'll take this novel on a ride. This novel will take us to a more distant destination than any other. Your mind. Similar to how we use charts in order to refine our travels we should automate the thought process using maps.

Mind maps, also known to be called databases, were used in recent learning philosophy research. It was found that the brain can store information and recall it easily from its memory by using phrases more than by trying large chunks of information.

Your mind uses keywords in order to uncover additional information and to create links between keywords.

The flow of ideas in mind charts is the key, and not drawing or typing. It makes it easy and faster to store, organize and retrieve information.

Make your brain happy, make mental maps to maximize your thinking.

Get it now

Next, you need to purchase a pen with paper.

Let's get started with something familiar. Please write your name and circle it in the middle. This is the primary keyword.

It should remind us of things.

Write new words around your name only with single words. This could be your family, friends (or colleagues), health, and any other thing that comes to mind.

These words are to be circled.

These are the divisions of keywords and should allow for more knowledge.

Some people just read the first few lines and then start to write new words. Don't do what is reasonable.

Next, you can add new branches like the names of family and friends.

Soon you will receive a diagram describing your life.

You will notice that there are links between the keywords.

Are your wellbeing, your job and your relationships and your emotions tied?

Before you complete the tab, continue adding divisions.

For marking whole sections or keywords, you can also use other colors.

A sentence can be represented using icons or illustrations. Focusing on information flow is the idea. Try to discover what works best for your situation.

Uses:

Anyone can use mental map to take notes, brainstorm ideas, plan and solve problems.

They can also be used in the creation of screenplays and novels, as well in the development of investment and company proposals.

Combine two keywords and you will have a whole new section on your mindmap. This method is great for generating ideas.

Computer Options

A great visual modelling tool is available, with options like an optimised notepad, colours, icon collection, PowerPoint Office, Outlook export solutions and Office. Google's "mindmap Software"

Mind Mapping helps you to perfect your presentations

Make your presentation complete with Mind Mapping.

It is too common for speakers to schedule speeches by using a few pages of notes with linear words.

We stay behind a microphone and read the feedback of our audience.

We talk in a monotone that encourages the audience to repeat their sentences. Heavily shaved necks and big heads are becoming a problem.

Is this really a good approach?

Yes, phrases aid in learning and recalling things without meaning. We are not only dull but also the brain is not flexible in design. Presentations also communicate information in a way that can be absorbed quickly by the brain.

Layouts are more successful when they include images, colors, patterns, connections, and associations.

These are the fundamental aspects that foster creativity, which is a primary learning mechanism. But how can you do it in a presentation?

Mind maps are great for structuring and systemizing.

Before you focus on the matter, map the main facts of the presentation.

Mind Maps are great for organizing and coordinating existing plans and ideas in an easy-to-remember way.

Next, consider who and what your message will benefit.

The mind map can include sections such case studies, research and inspiration. With this mental mapping, you should consistently transform the main words and ideas. Make sure to use hard-to-use data as support for your viewpoints and suggestions.

Your central image must include the topic. Branch images should represent the topics you are discussing.

A mental map will help you see your position clearly and efficiently within a larger context.

Be Courageous

Use pictures and colors

It is one way to best communicate your point using images, colours symbols, etc.

The complex and engaging display is made more interesting by the visual stimuli.

A long list with boring information can quickly become a colorful, memorable and highly organized diagram that reflects your natural thinking process and encourages synergistic thinking.

Thus, your Mind Map will include a division for ideas and thoughts to make your presentation interesting, engaging, memorable.

The Practice Is Perfect

It is important to keep one branch on your mind map focused on the method you feel most necessary to ensure your allocated time is not used.

You can also use Mind Maps to decide how long to spend on each topic.

How can I help? Demonstrations can be made much more simple thanks to state-of-the art graphics.

Computerised Mind Maps can now be imported to PowerPoint with Mind Mapping software (e.g. Tony Buzan's iMindMap).

Don't be tempted to create a long list with PowerPoint phrases or sentences that do not interest your audience.

Engagement with your audience, another critical element of performance, is also important.

It can be achieved by the creation of a mental roadmap. You communicate this knowledge to your community and invite them for suggestions or opinions.

Instead, encourage your attendees to take notes during your presentation. It demands that the audience thinks independently and encourages active participation.

Therefore, the audience is more likely to benefit from your presentation.

Mind Maps can be used to help participants break the linear tradition of noting down and aid them in making appropriate associations and absorbing more information.

Now, you need to plan a great event.

Mind Mapping For Focus

Mind maps make this easier for those who find it difficult to plan or remember information.

Mind mapping has been shown by research to improve memory, solve difficult problems, and allow individuals to organize and understand large sections of information. This technique will connect two subjects that can provide depth to your discussion.

Mind mapping is useful for writers, editors, and anyone who works in writing.

Research also shows that mind mapping can improve students' ability to do assignments and complete exercises.

You can use them in your work, career planning and everyday life.

Brain maps enable you to coordinate many more than simple information about any region.

It is easy.

For the first step, write your main topic onto a blank sheet.

From the main subject to the most important categories, draw lines (arrows, boxes or any other type of line you choose).

Drawing pictures next to them can improve recall.

Start to create subtopics. Brainstorm and use free association. Don't be afraid of making mistakes. If you feel the need, add categories or subtopics.

It's only for your convenience.

While you may think you are complete when you have nothing to add, you will often find that there is more to be done if we get back to what we have done.

After you have completed the chart, it can be easily copied and/or colour coded.

Read through what you have discovered and talk about the assumptions.

If you feel still overwhelmed, keep the map beside you and return to the map in a few days or hours.

It is important to not let advancements end with the mind.

Once you've made one and are clear about where you want to go, get on with it!

A plan of action or to-do list is necessary.

Be positive and don't let anyone make you feel hard.

You have the option to make mind maps in your newspaper. Or you could choose to use them as a reminder that you are often using them. You can write them on scrappaper and drop them off. I use other pages to print, and I use my back for mine. Another tip:

To make it easy to find them later, you should place the finished maps into a three-ring folder.

Mind maps are a good way to get many ideas across without being stuck.

After your work is complete, you can read it all and then start to create something that incorporates your most effective ideas.

Is your brain on hot-air working on project planning? Mind mapping helps you to stay calm.

Project planning is an integral part of any project.

Every project requires timely and successful project execution. Proper project preparation, therefore, is necessary.

Project planning elements are time estimation for various work segments, time plan for the different work layers, monitoring and surveillance, separation of the important from the unimportant, and meeting the deadline.

It is being ready for unexpected events or contingencies and taking correctional actions to ensure that the case does NOT get out of hand.

All of these require planning.

Mind Mapping can help in so many areas of work and cover a vast array of services. It can be very useful in tracing your path to details and working out the details. Mind Maps can be used for illustrating the different work phases. You can give your ideas a free rein and work on the main task from the first to the last stages.

The Mind Map of each unit will be displayed when you divide them.

You can define multiple elements of project plan so that the team who will be responsible for each aspect of the projects can work together.

Brainstorming will enable you to get different points of views and offer suggestions.

It also includes feedback and suggestions from the Manager as well as full participation.

Each person is involved in designing and executing a project. This creates a sense a purpose and encourages teamwork.

Individual brainstorming might also be possible on the main tasks and goals of each section of the group.

These issues can then be compared, and linked to brainstorming results.

It can be used to help any part or job to be objectively, dynamically and continuously analysed by Mind Map. This includes repetitive and necessary tasks as well as the more complex.

Mind Map is a straightforward and important tool that taps into our brain's parallel processing capacity. Any level of task success can be addressed most imaginatively.

Mind Map uses links and associations to give new perspectives.

It is possible to combine various elements of your Project Plan into one cohesive mind map when different work divisions are clearly identified and fully explored. It is possible to see all aspects of the project at once and monitor every stage of its execution.

The formal listing of tasks will not be able to cover this type of process. We are an end unto ourselves, and we don't encourage interaction between the elements.

Mind Map can help you to manage and rework every phase of your project planning. You also get a view of the synchronisation across the various elements.

Chapter 8: Visual Mapping Methods & Types

Mind mapping is only one of many ways to organize ideas and information. A structured process allows you to absorb and retain information in the most effective and efficient manner that imitates the cognitive thinking patterns within your brain.

This section will provide information on various types of mind-mapping that you could use. Also, we will cover computer-generated methods and hand drawn mind maps that you can integrate into your mind map exercises.

Visual mapping types

These seven maps can be used to show the information. These maps will vary depending on the structure and purpose of the information being studied, your goals & objective, and how you intend to use them.

*Cyclical mapping: Key terms used to correlate within phases in a cycle.

*Converging mapping: This is used to connect causes that have a single result.

*Radialmaps: These are mind map structures that have subtopics floating off a central word/image.

*Hierarchical charts: These are used in order to show key terms or diminishing portions of a larger topic.

*Comparisonmaps: These maps can be used to compare 2 or more things. The central interlocking section represents the objects shared characteristics or parts.

*Interactingmaps: These are concept-map structures that can connect to each other in various ways.

*Linear map: These flowcharts correspond to the linear phases in a process and have a beginning or a end.

Mind mapping methods

Below are two mind mapping options that can be used in order to convey the information you have just learned. Each method is different and each has its pros and cons. You should consider your objectives and your learning goals before choosing the right method.

It is possible for you to choose which method you prefer based on the amount of time and resources available.

Hand-drawn maps of the mind

The beauty of hand drawn mind maps is that they can enhance your understanding and way of thinking about the topics that you are studying. Here are some of the benefits and drawbacks of hand drawn mindmaps:

Benefits

Hand-drawn mind maps are flexible in that you can stretch, shrink and bend the map however you like. This improves the organic structure and makes the mind map easier to recall.

A hand drawn map is personal and very individual. This personal touch corresponds to how you think and allows for you to better absorb the information.

Demerits

The space that you leave on the piece of paper in which you draw your maps is a key factor. This can mean that you may need to map out the information at the edges of what you have.

Hand-drawn maps of the mind can take time. It can take up to a long time to make a hand-drawn mind map. Computer-generated mind maps take about the same amount.

Computer Generated Mind Maps

This mind mapping method is gaining a lot more attention in recent years. There are now more mind mapping software apps than ever. Each month seems to bring a new participant in the market. Each piece of software, online or offline, has its own strengths and flaws. We are not going to discuss the details. Instead, we will compare modern mind mapping software against hand-drawn maps.

Merits

Computer generated mindmaps can be multi-dimensional, expandable, collapsible, or assembled quickly.

Weaknesses

Computer-generated mind maps are not flexible and personal. It might not be possible to visualize the things you have in mind.

3D mind mapping

Here are the 3D Mind Mapping Software Applications currently available. These packages can immerse and transport you into the world of content. They allow you understand information from the perspective an insider.

*Nelements
*Topicscape

Online mind mapping courses

Here's a list of online mind-mapping and flow-charting tools that you can use in order to create your mind maps. Each package is different, so you need to find the online software that meets all your requirements.

*Gliffy
*FlowChart
*Mapul
*Mind42
*CoMapping
*Mindomo
*Bubbl.us
*MindMeister

There are less-known mapping packages
Here are some of these less-popular mind mapping and concept mapping software applications you can find online. These software programs are not as well-known, but some of them are very innovative and provide many fascinating features.
*MYmap
*Mind Genius
*Pocket Mindmap
*Mind Visualizer
*TheBrain
*Cayra
*BrainMine
*MindPad
*HeadCase
*MindPlan
*i2Brain
*MindCad
*SparkSpace
Mind Mapping Study Strategies
Preparation: Prior to class
Make sure you know beforehand what the topic of the class will be and what textbook chapters you will need. Once you have this information, take some time to

skim through the chapters. You will be able to identify important points of information that are most relevant to your thinking. Once you are done, begin to prepare your mindmap using your favorite mind-mapping program. The purpose of this stage, is to create a mind map that includes the main headings and subheadings. These should be arranged and organized in a way which helps you better understand the topic.

Expansion of the class:

Bring your tablet, notebook, and laptop along to the class to add additional notes while you listen to lectures.

Assimilation - After class

This is a good idea to do the same thing as before. To begin, read through the topic section of your handouts. Keep reading the topic chapter of your handouts or textbook. Then, add personal opinions, keywords headings and subheadings to your mind map. After the mindmap is assembled you can include memory triggers. Start by adding the following information:

*Memorable photos to your main headings.

*Links that take you to important files on your computer, like Excel spreadsheets or PowerPoints

*Links from your tasks and/or calendar

*Links to relevant websites and other information

*Add important symbols that will help identify particular parts of content

*You can transform your mind map by adding various colors to your branches

*Bind font differentiation by adjusting the size, style, feel and size of words

*Include highlights to specific sections to highlight their importance/relationship

*Adjust your lines for a more organic look.

*Adjust word boxes structure by changing them into rectangles or circles. Once you're done, you might find something similar:

General guidelines

It is important to not strictly adhere to the content structure in the textbook or notes you are summarizing through your mindmap. Mindmaps are not designed to regurgitate information, as the lecturer or textbook would have it. A mind map is not a way to memorize or recall information. You may find it useful to link topics within different chapters in your mindmap. Or, you may choose to divide a topic in two to better understand what is being taught. It is important to compile all of the work for your semester (including your essays, lecture notes, textbooks notes, and tests) into a single mindmap. By bringing all of the information together in one place, you can create a global view of your topic area. However, you shouldn't just randomly throw the information together. It is much more beneficial to actually link the information together, mix ostensibly unrelated data, and structure them in a way which helps you better understand the topic. Your final mindmap should reflect what you think about the subject. It shouldn't be just a summary of what your lecturer has presented.

Exam study tips with mind maps

Once your mind map has been created, it is time to begin studying for the exams. This is the point where you should have all of your information in the mindmap. It is now time to go through each and every branch in detail, and to incorporate the information into a long-term memory.

You can read the entire mind map.

The ability to piece together all of the branches of your mindmap in the most effective and efficient manner possible. Through this process you will slowly develop the ability to create a photographic memories. You'll be amazed at how quickly you remember the details you need to excel in this subject area when you sit for your exams.

Below is a description of the process as well as a guide to how to apply it.

Read

Select one branch and take it through your mind. Pay close attention to the images and font sizes as well symbols, highlights, colors, highlights, and other details while you read the branch. This is how you can link these physical landmarks and the content of your mind map. In general, the more that you focus and stay focused on this process the more productive it will be. This stage might be best if you set a time limit. This is an accelerated learning strategy, and time restrictions are vital because they will cause your brain to be more effective in analyzing the information.

Recall

After having read through the entire first branch of your mindmap thoroughly, you are able to then recall it from memory. Picture the branch you just read in your mind with your eyes closed. Think of all the landmarks you can think of, such as font size, highlight, symbols and colors.

Imagine that you are walking on a familiar path. This is a comfortable, relaxed way to go. Begin to visualize this branch in your head as you move along. Once you have done so, begin to describe the journey aloud. You'll notice an increase in neural associations as you become more emotionally involved with the process. This stage should be completed within a set time frame to make sure you are able to move through the whole thing in the proper time.

Review

Once you're finished with your mental journey go back to your mind map branch and glaze over it. Pay attention to the sub-branches or segments that are most difficult to remember. You may find it useful to highlight those words or subbranches that are hard to remember at this stage. This will help you to recall the ideas as you read through the branches again. Before you start the next phase of the process, take a few moments to review the entire branch. It is also important that you set a time limit.

Test

Once you have reviewed the branch, you will be able to begin testing your knowledge. You have 3 options to test you knowledge.

*Answering question: This is when you ask yourself questions related to the branch you have just studied and then see if it can be answered. If you find a difficult question to answer, simply refer to your mind map to find it. You can then answer the question in your own words. Following this method will allow you to easily locate the answer in a mind map and make it easier to find it again.

*Sketching branch: You can quickly draw the particular branch in your mind map on a piece. This will stimulate your physical or cognitive intelligence and enable you to quickly absorb the material. While sketching your mindmap, pay close attention to colors. Font differentiations, symbology, and branch thickness are all important. It is important to keep your auditory senses stimulated by discussing your sketch aloud. A time limit should be set for the entire process.

*Explaining mindmap branch: Only mind mapping software can do this. It allows you expand and collapse branches. For the first level of each branch, collapse them all. Once you've recalled the 2nd level, expand it. Then try to remember the chunks and subheadings that are within the 3rd Layer. Continue the process until all branches have been successfully expanded to the fourth and fifth, sixth, seventh, and seventh levels. As you work through this process, it's okay to go backwards and forth in order to remember difficult bits of information. Make sure you highlight any sub-branches that are difficult to recall, so you can revisit them later.

You can repeat the 3R+T Procedure.

After you are done with one branch move on to the next. You can either go clockwise (or anticlockwise) and continue rotating through the remainder of the branches. You will continue this process for seven consecutive days until you have fully assimilated information. Each day, make sure to reduce the time between each branch.

It is quite remarkable to see that a complete 500 page book can be consolidated in a matter of days using the

3R+T process. It also gives you an impressive 88% recall rate.

Developing Your Visual Awareness

Visual thinking is a skill that requires you to recognize patterns every day. These patterns contain the answers to your problems and obstacles as you think visual. To recognize these patterns, however, you first need to train your eyes to better understand your surroundings.

It can take time to build your visual thinking muscles. You will be able to see patterns in your life and understand how they affect your thinking.

It's all in your eyes

We'll be focusing our attention on improving your vision awareness since we're talking about visual thinking. It is important that you realize that your awareness can be sharpened through all your sensory systems. You actually gain more information when you use multiple sensory organs to enhance your awareness. This will help you to better understand your situations and problems.

It was not uncommon for early explorers to find unusual things in their environment during the period of global discovery. These amazing things hadn't been found before. Therefore, they had to capture the essence in a visual format that others could understand. This resulted in the creation of sketches that helped to depict animals, like the elephants shown below.

The illustrations are very odd looking. They look more similar to horses or donkeys without trunks, rather than elephants. This shows that even experts can have difficulties visualizing things they haven't before. The images can give readers a visual clue about the animal's look. Consider what it would look like if the artist created a graph of the animal instead of an image, such as the one shown below.

The graph presented here does not have the same visual impact as the earlier images. However, it presents details in a unique and useful way. The lesson is that not all visual communications methods work the same. Be aware of which visual communication method you use to communicate your ideas.

Chapter 9: Optimizing 6 Meetings

Do you ever feel lonely? Are you lonely to be in your own corner? Do you hate making decisions? Go to a MEETING and you'll be able: - Make new friends, – Create schedules, Impress your coworkers, And - Write notes on your Palm or in your notebook. - Look smart. - Approve with a smile. All this all during work hours. MEETINGS offer a practical alternative work.

Advertisement spotted in a firm

These meetings represent one of the most "time-consuming" activities. This is where 20 or 25% of our work time goes. Due to the reduced opportunities of simultaneous presence with our coworkers due to the 35 hour work week, productivity tips are more essential than ever. It doesn't matter if it is formal or informal, the meeting time can still be cut with simple tools. Let's look at mind maps again.

The constraints meetings

Meetings can be limited by many factors: time synchronization between participants, the definition of objectives, and others.

We need to make sure that everyone is available at the right time and at the right place. There are also other constraints like the availability rooms with all equipment, laptops and video projectors, as well as flipcharts (with pen and markers)! Blackout of rooms and availability of other places

sYMPTOMS

We hear from colleagues almost every day: "Too many meetings"," I did not get the minutes",,"I was not at previous meeting", etc.

There are many signs and symptoms that can lead to excessive meetings, loss, mistrust, ineffectiveness, and poor adherence. Participants are frustrated by the lack of attention, inefficiency, and frustrations. Beyond the agenda, we won't be discussing the expected results and their achievement. You also feel the lack in preparation for the next meeting.

These are the complaints we hear most often. What are the causes?

Causes

The list of causes could go on and on.

* poor preparation, agenda that was not established before the meeting, unspecified purposes, participants more or lesser concerned, weak motivation (we assume we will waste our precious time);

* no or very few working methods, unattractive supportive (bulky, repetitive reports that nobody has ever seen before, or will never have time for), indigestible dashboards decisions were not taken (sometimes, there was not even an updated date selected for the next meeting).);

* There is no common thread. This causes frequent digressions when it comes to the agenda items.

* While meetings are often regarded as a rite of passage that provides rhythm to the organization's activities, they are not required. It is not something that we do out of habit. It may serve as an excuse for participation, the search to justifications

and not actions. How often do people try to justify themselves? Instead, they should look at the facts and see if we are average or excellent.

* Finally, we tend rely passively to the facilitator. This long list is easily summarized by the fact, that many decisions are never used.

The cost of the lost time can be calculated in thousands without considering transport and accommodation costs. It is possible save 10% on time spent in meetings.

There are several options available to help with the above-mentioned causes.

The standard answer

The Monday morning ritual gathering is the typical response. It's held regardless how important the topics are. It's a Council of the Wise in a few places, but it has a huge impact on the lives of many other organizations. It is important for its friendliness, and for the chance to exchange ideas. Sometimes the list contains a few simple items. The work completed is complete by the report.

Participants should wait for the reports to know the details and take appropriate action.

Regular participants feel like they have a privilege. This is because they get to see the world firsthand and can then consume information without having to be involved. Each person's creativity may also be used in informal settings, or where the viewpoints on the subject are different.

Psychological is another common response. The problem is that we often waste a lot time in meetings. A simple example is: How many people are motivated at the end to change their behavior after a meeting? Check back in a few weeks to see how many have reverted to their previous ways.

Why is it so difficult for people change? The answer is very simple. People and organizations cannot make changes because they are unable to learn from their mistakes. Chris Kennedy said that we are so good in hiding the truth that often we don't even realize we are doing it.

The defenses that we have adopted are unconsciously carried on. We can adapt to the extraordinary complexity of the world by recognising our reactions. To be able change, one must first know where you are. We don't know how to move about in the conceptual space of a meeting. It's possible to draw cards and make them easily. These cards offer many benefits.

The art card heuristics act as animation tools

The cards can almost be used in every type of meeting. We can recognize four types.

* Pre-arranged meetings
* Unscheduled meetings
* forgotten meetings,
* Meetings canceled.

Even if we think there should be scheduled meetings we know there is always the possibility of something unexpected. We can be more efficient if we follow these tips.

Our memory capacities are more frequently used than anywhere else in meetings. We know that about:

* From 10 to 20% of what she has read;

* 20-30% to 300% of what she hears
* From 30 to 50%, she sees.
* Between 50-60% of the things she sees or hears simultaneously
* 60% to 80 % of what it reformulates
* 80 to 100% if it acts and gets involved

Some suggestions are made for the facilitator

* use numerous visual aids (tables, transparencies, films, etc.);
* Include the group as many times as possible.

Flipcharts are the MIRROR in our group. The flipchart finds itself there, and it sees it moving. The first agenda card is used to build the card.

This card will be used to prepare for the meeting. Each participant may take the agenda card and use it as a draft. You can share the agenda card with everyone who is invited to your meeting if you have an intranet. If you don't have an intranet, or just email, you can send the agenda in the format of a card. The recipients can use it as a note transport.

An organizer can prepare a larger map that will serve to guide the meeting. Depending on available funds, the flipchart can be used to draw and color. My personal preference is to have the main color of the tree. During the meeting, the main color is changed so that everyone can see their contributions.

If possible, the session secretary will complete and sign the computerized paper on a Microcomputer. It will become a photocopy shortly after the meeting ends. Emailing within an hour of the meeting will be possible, too. With a report that is exported to word processing, you can always double the information circuit. We were stunned to discover that our colleagues retained the card report and not just took linear notes. This not only takes up less space, but also offers remarkable capabilities for synthesis. Some prefer to keep the old format as it provides them with comfort.

The cards can be used to help groups learn and work together. How? What is 'Or?' Cascading cards: Different branches of a motherboard refers to other cards. Daughter cards refer to their own cards.

The map will grow at the next meeting.

Scheduled Meetings

Despite French law that limits work hours to 35 per hour, the pressure on us is rising to finish all our work. It is also more important than ever to have productive meetings.

Frame the goal

Instead of making the points distributed in a linear manner, let us give our participants an Agenda Card with one branch per Point.

Only the main limbs are present. The objective of the meeting is for this tree to grow by giving it ramifications. The meeting will start with the group constitution phase.

Collect ideas

We now enter the production phase. It is much more fun to allow ourselves to use the color marker, the small drawings. You can also add your ideas by using a live projector to help make the map even more interesting. The global map, which will be visible from all angles, will always be in sight. This will give meaning and interest to the actions of all.

Without orienting the participants in a certain direction, it's possible to examine the subject by going branch-by-branche. It will take small steps to formalize and listen to all the ideas in the assembly.

Our ideas will be based on our individual expressions and the goals we have for the particular branch. It is possible. Our card can have the same size as a piece of paper or a wall diagram. We can use a roll on paper tablecloth to make more space. The collective card will be enhanced by the contributions from the entire group.

Make assumptions

"If it does this, it will do that." This card can be used to visually compare different hypotheses and it also allows them to be placed on the same supporting. This tree-treemap that has just been created can be refined to maintain consistency and calibrate certain hypotheses. 360@ update of several solutions is possible because of the physical availability of this card.

Understanding them in detail reduces the chances of miscommunications between participants. The visual support during meetings is an additional benefit. It pushes back the limit of short-term memory (6 to 7 elements may be simultaneously stored). As people work together, the map expands and develops at the same rate. It is a visible sign that the ideas are weaving in front and among the "weavers", those who participate in the collective project.

This card offers a significant service, as it allows one to turn back during a meeting. No problem. We can easily connect to the thread that we were in before. You will find that there is a lot of backtracking involved in meeting progress, just like when you search the Internet. With the map, you can start quickly and then come back to the exact point where you were.

Decide

To create an action program, three simple questions must be answered.

* Who does what

* When?
* When are you going to do it?

For more information, please see Chapters 7 and 6.

Impromptu meetings

You suddenly realized, while having a casual conversation with someone you don't know, that important topics were being addressed. Never have we been caught by our manager in the corridor to discover a new task for us to complete without knowing everything?

To concentrate

As the discussion moves from banal, to professional let's concentrate on the key ideas for capturing the maximum data. Let's not pay attention to the importance of our conversation partner, nor the location or their environment.

Take note of any medium

This will help improve our memory. Create a map. In a very small area, you can add more information. We will be able to find the best connections between the keywords that are being identified. Let's borrow some pen and put our thoughts on the back cover of an envelope. It is important to note what is being said at that moment.

To ask questions

It is crucial to ask the interlocutor about his intentions in this informal meeting. It's a German proverb: "Wer fragte der fuhrt", which reminds us that

"The game is won by the questioner"

Start a mindmap as soon you can

A way to store the majority of our data on minimal media, paper or any other medium, is essential. Many of our colleagues write on their phones or on the palms of their electronic assistants.

To be certain you understand, repeat the process.

It is not easy to understand the message when there are noises around and conditions that aren't ideal. Rearranging what our interlocutor tells us will help. It is even better that our scribbled paper will be helpful. With the additional replies we receive, our draft of the card will be refined. This will allow you to add relationships onto your map.

Send a summary Text

We will all be closing down business back at the office or, at the very least, providing a summary from our impromptu meeting. We will depend on the pencil card and any notes we took "on-the fly". This will be used as a "meeting' record. We can also use this record to update our workload if the meeting results in unplanned additional tasks.

When we make our map on a PC, we can put dates on our report that has just been sent to our contact.

Cultural convergence meeting

Mind maps can also be used for deep facilitation of understanding and sharing the perspectives of others.

Many of the rules in any project are "Unofficial", meaning there are implicit understandings that not everyone shares or acknowledges.

These rules can also be clarified and communicated by cards.

When a group emerges from the group, often the dominant culture is stronger or more dominant. They abandon those less dominant or destabilized members. They believe that if it is necessary, they can.

Group awareness

Our first witness comes from a French government that started a project several years ago. One of these axes focused on improving reception.

Two groups of managers met in the same setting, one week apart. The same location, the same animator, the same goal: to improve reception. The only thing that has been different between the two groups is the fact that the former used the mindmap to facilitate their meeting.

The first meeting was unsuccessful. The critics were coming down.

The facilitator changed his tactics and started using the mind maps in the second session.

Two homogeneous, similar groups started almost at the exact same time. The results were amazing: there were more ideas from older people and a much better atmosphere.

The mind map also showed a glitch that the first group couldn't see:

communication issues were caused jointly by two different messaging systems, two electronic calendars, and certain other factors.

Crisis management

New York firefighters provide an excellent example of how mind maps can be crucial and even vital.

They cannot afford to be mistaken when they're faced with emergency situations. They have to act fast. Mind maps have become an integral part of their everyday life. How? 'Or?' What?

They knew in just a few seconds what resources they could depend on during the September 11th attacks.

A mind map can contain information at various levels. It can also be used to reclassify the information so that they are readable together. They could clearly see the issue and the possible solutions. The map became an invaluable tool to help the group evaluate its progress towards achieving their goal.

This map can be viewed in three ways: by region, by detail and global.

* The fire commander can see a general overview of the resources available at any moment. Firefighters, ambulances and access, firefighters, and nurses are all available.

* Zones that are materialized with clouds on a chart can be used as a guide to help identify a group or individual visual elements (color spots/pastilles, etc.). This information will also allow for you to determine how many resources (trucks; firefighters; ambulances; nurses) are available on your south side.

* The reading of a tree is described in detail: How many firefighters are present at the south-facing door?

Chapter 10: Feelings Can Sometimes Be The Most Powerful But Also The Most Detrimental Aspect Of Life.

Day by day, emotions drive our decisions. We embrace new possibilities and take advantage of them.

We weep, because we have been wounded. And, because we care we make sacrifices.

Our emotions are the foundation of our opinions, beliefs, and behaviour.

However, if emotions aren't controlled quickly or wrongly felt, we may make poor decisions that will later be regretted.

Between dangerous extremes, our feelings can change. Be too extreme and you will get angry.

Don't go too far right and you'll feel like you are in a state that is full of joy.

Emotions, as with all other aspects of our lives, can be best viewed with a sense balance and rational insight.

We shouldn't fall for love or jump with joy after hearing good news.

These are the most wonderful things in your life. These are extreme negative emotions that must be managed with caution.

Negative emotions such rage or envy can become out of control very quickly after triggers.

These types of emotions may become root-like and slowly take over the mind.

Ever met someone who was always angry or hostile.

They did not grow like this, but allowed the feelings to flow through them for so long, that it all seemed all too natural.

How do we not allow our emotions to get in the way of our success?

Follow these six steps for emotional control and rationality.

Don't react right away.

It can be dangerous to respond quickly to emotional triggers.

You are certain to regret something later.

Take a deep inhale and calm the overwhelming momentum. Next, you will need to refute the trigger by using your emotional argument.

Allow your body to relax for 5 minutes.

Be sure to calm down and realize that this is temporary.

Ask God For Guidance

Trusting God in the darkest hour is our salvation grace. Whatever your faith, you can overcome obstacles by building a healthy partnership with the holy Universe.

Because you believe the power to create and will be taught by it.

Help you understand why certain things are happening.

If you're feeling emotional burdened, close all your eyes and imagine a positive solution.

Shop for a Healthy Outlet.

Now, it's time to be able to feel free.

Feelings should not be kept inside. Reach out to someone you trust and let them know what happened.

Listening to someone else's opinion can help broaden your conscience. Keep a journal to record your emotions and then transfer them to the paper.

Many people find that it helps them to perform vigorous exercises like kickboxing or martial art to unleash their emotions.

To restore calm, others meditate and sing. Do whatever activity works best for you in order to let go of any pent up feelings.

Check out the Larger Picture.

Each situation in our lives, regardless of how it turns out, serves a higher purpose.

Wisdom is the ability of seeing the moment in the past and to see the greater meaning of any situation.

Although it may be difficult to grasp at first, you will soon see the bigger picture.

Even during the most difficult emotions, you can trust that you will soon see the end goal.

Replace Your Thoughts.

Negative emotions are a way to create negative loops and repetitive thoughts.

You can replace any negative emotion you have with another one if you come across it. For the ultimate solution, think of someone who makes you smile, or about an event that made it so.

Forgive the Causes Of Your Anger

Your emotional triggers can be your best friend.

Anger can quickly build if your friend does the "thing she does", or you forget something.

It is possible to forgive and get rid off your resentment, jealousy, or fury. You have learned to let go your anger, jealousy and fury. You accept people for who they are and don't grow your emotions. By forgiving, you are free from any strong sentiments.

Every second of the day, our emotions rise through us, reminding us of our ardent nature.

If we allow our negative feelings to run rampant in our heads, then we will always choose wrong actions.

A few simple steps can help to prevent emotional turmoil and keep you from burning.

You'll be grateful you could be your own emotional master when the moment passes. Emotional control is yours.

Mind Maps, Movement

A visual diagram is useful for organizing and facilitating transition. It's an easy way to figure out what to act in a difficult situation.

Tony Buzan designed mind maps. This simple technique can be used to create radiating lines that connect the themes of your difficulty or decision, and write them in the center of your text.

Every new topic will contain other parts as you learn more concepts. It is possible to link ideas by using diagrams or colourful types.

The visual charts give you a glimpse at your emotions. It takes the focus off of the usual checklist which contributes to a linear focus.

On one piece, you can create a representation that reflects your thought on the subject.

This approach allows you to think "outside of the door." This method allows you to store a lot more material on one sheet of paper. You can find it on the internet.

Use mind-map to track your mood and see the changes in your environment as you go through your different options. You can alter your mental condition or feel immediately by changing your body shape. It may be something to do with your posture. Many people find it beneficial to go for a swim or to dance to live musical to alter their perceptions and actions.

The movement has the purpose of changing how you feel. It can increase your creativity by changing your energy level.

Your walk can seem to trap your emotions. Notice any friction or stress areas.

Learn from others, and practice. Then copy them and you'll be able to feel the difference in how your walking affects your emotions.

It's easy to notice if your emotions are different about certain situations if the stance you choose is more relaxed or firmer.

Walking is believed to be a form meditation. When you walk, new ideas flood your mind and solve previously unsolved issues.

Combining them is a winning combination. It can help you generate ideas and encourage imagination through regular exercise, a mindmap and other methods.

Mind Maps to Manage Time

Recently I've introduced to maps which I start to use to improve time management.

Tony Buzan books are something I've enjoyed. Map techniques have helped me to see the benefits. If you read this book, you will see that mind mapping can enhance your time management.

We usually have a main theme that is familiar to those unfamiliar with it and many branches beyond it.

It is broken down into smaller details by smaller branches. Its strength comes from its ability brainstorm and visualize the overall goal the central subject represents.

My time management has been a process that I have used in several stages. I am currently using mind maps to improve efficiency.

I start by keeping a notepad or a diary with tasks to complete. I had to determine what I would do, make a chart, and finish the checklist before the end of the day. Everything else was added to the list.

I realized then that although things get busier, they didn't necessarily have to be done all by ourselves.

It was more important to delegate small, routine tasks when I had more.

If there aren't enough people to do more mundane work, I may also consider outsourcing.

The 80/20 Law allows 80% to be drawn from 20% or more of our jobs.

The most efficient return tasks will make us more efficient.

While time is critical, it's also directly linked to money. If we spend our time well, we can be successful and financially secure.

This was my goal, so I went on to thematic list. I want to achieve multiple goals.

However, there are small steps that I need to take.

I was required to choose from the various measures that I wanted to undertake every day.

I understood how to organise my goals.

The amount of work that I have left to complete is distracting me from the hustle and bustle of my job.

While these are things that keep me busy, they are not necessarily necessary. These items may be removed from your list without any consequences.

What I like most about mental maps? The central theme is always the subject. This is a must for all activities.

We can see its importance and the reasons why it is not. The left-hand conceptual architecture of research can be seen one side.

Take into consideration the quality of your job.

When you are looking at charts, it is important to focus on the central theme. It is this power that makes you more effective with visual maps.

Mind Map your Ways from Unemployed to A New Job

People are increasingly facing a global financial crisis. Many people lose their jobs and need to find new employment to make sufficient money.

It would be wonderful to have a mental plan for a fresh job.

You are likely to already be able to create a mapping. To get the job you desire, use this ability.

The key to a successful job search is your ability to organize large quantities of information. For both your personal and professional information, you must establish order and structure. TODAY! Keep in mind that you don't need to feel overwhelmed.

Answer three questions in order to find a better job.

Can you make yourself visible on paper in a visually compelling format?

How do I plan my path through an interview?

More mental map tools are allowing you to import RSS Feeds directly into your map.

It is helpful to have RSS feeds with work that you are able submit.

Simply open and edit your mindmap. Now, all you have to do is open your mind map and update it.

It makes it possible to surf the net. More work can result in less time.

Most people don't have the expertise to do this job (this is by definition).

This means that your approach must be professional but different. However, you should not be intimidating.

It's not easy to take the drastic steps needed in difficult times.

Yes, that's right.

A mindmap should outline who you are in business.

Be confident. Do something you won't be able to do for most people. Make a personal plan for yourself. Send one your future employer.

Your transition to getting the interview will take less than one minute.

A mind map can be a powerful tool. All information is displayed on a large screen (it is concisely presented) and you display yourself in full color (you stickout), rather than in black and white ("you look out").

Add a company emblem. The content must relate to the job.

There are no words you need anymore.

It is essential to grasp that the diagram must always be easily understood and simple.

The user needs to be able immediately to grasp the meaning of what is displayed. There's no need for confusion.

Avoid using too many (bright!) colours. Be skilled!

All of this depends on the company that you send the map.

Map Your Way through the interview

The map is made (often before you meet). Preparation makes up ninety per cent.

Include the following information on your document: interview company date-add key information about your questions on a specific table.

A clear map is essential. Talk about it without being shy.

The information should be managed by the other party.

Displaying map information should be displayed in one color only, according to me. Because you are a practitioner, it is important to not act like someone who enjoys painting.

If you believe in the potential, mind mapping could be described. Or you can make a list of all the company information you've received!

I know you'll be impressed by the way your future colleague summarises and provides an overview.

Mind Mapping is a way to build trust and communicate effectively.

I've always believed that there is a special, unspoken connection between people in our nervous sistem and that if you act in a certain manner, your spouse will respond.

I believe my confusion stems primarily from my mistaken belief that my counterpart would always be able to respond with positive communication and positive actions.

The argument is that not everyone at the parent's house received the same basic instruction in social skills so as adults we don't all have the exact same responses to certain situations.

It can lead to a lack of productive communication at work or at home.

Mind Map's effectiveness in personal and professional training will be evident. This will allow you the opportunity to learn about how multicultural societies affect your thinking and feelings.

Effective communication skills are the cornerstone of empowering the workforce, encouraging productivity and strengthening employer/employee partnerships.

Employers want workers with high levels of conversation skills as they are the most important personal attributes.

Mind Map Mentoring has been shown to significantly increase self-worth in individuals who use it to improve communication skills.

Communication takes many forms during difficult times.

It is a very inexpensive communication method, but it can be vital and valuable in helping people to regain their self-motivation.

The courage to show your integrity and selflessness by offering constructive assistance and generously giving your time can help others.

It can seem as hostile to preserve constructive contact, but it is true human nature to show concern for the weaker.

The main question regarding effective verbal communication lies in the ability to silence your inner thoughts while listening actively to the person infront of you, so that you can hear what he/she has to share.

It is necessary to be open-minded and willing to listen before a person has an opposing opinion and can have a constructive discussion.

Some of our inner feelings or beliefs were suppressed by all manner of external pressures.

It can be counterproductive, as individuals can become disconnected from who and what is important to them.

Mind Mapping can be a very effective brain training system. It encourages people to talk in structured workshops. People realize that what they have to say is understandable and appreciated for its uniqueness.

It is essential that you build trust by mapping out your mind.

Thought mapping, a beautiful method that encourages self-growth as well as personal progress, is called thought mapping.

Once you have experienced active listening that is non-judgmental and constructive-which is an important part of positive learning-you will learn to appreciate the value of listening carefully to the words of others around you!

It allows for better communication and harmony between colleagues, friends, and family.

Mind mapping (also known as concept mapping and thinking mapping) is a great tool to help remove negative stereotypes and misperceptions that are preventing personal growth.

Mind Mapping facilitates positive conversations and leads to meaningful discussions.

It is possible to trust that you will understand this concept in good health.

Chapter 11: Exercises

Summer

For your convenience, all exercises have been combined. Other exercises can be used to practice mind mapping.

Budget Exercises

Grab a piece of paper and a pen. Or, you can use the mindmap software. I have listed several steps in exercise 1. These do not have to be done in a specific order. It's not necessary to do them in a particular order.

Exercise 1: To start this exercise, create a Budget. It can be as straightforward or as complex as your heart desires.

Here we go.

1. Main topic - Budget. This information should be placed in the middle section of the paper.

2. Subtopics are a 5 minute time frame in which you can simply write whatever comes to your mind regarding the main topic.

3. Lower level topics: take 5 minutes to look at the subtopics.

4. Add lower level topics if you wish.

5. Take a while to look over the notes you have made. A subtopic may need to be a lower level topic. Or, a topic that is lower in level might make a better subtopic.

6. Start by adding lines from your main topic to subtopics. After that, move on to lower-level topics. You may need to wrap the line around some connections.

7. You can embellish the map to make your map more memorable. If you're working on paper, add color, shape, and so forth. You will be able to use different fonts.

8. You can review your budget tomorrow to make any changes you wish.

Now that you have created your mindmap, you can use it to organize your budget. It's okay for you to think about how you could have done this better. There is no right and wrong way. Just the way you find useful.

Exercise 2 -- Pick a primary topic and create an outline. It could be anything.

It would be interesting to see what your thoughts are. You can mail it to:

To-Do Exercises

It is now your turn to make a To Do list.

Exercise 1: Make a To Do-List. It can be as simple, complex or fancy as your heart desires.

1. You can take a minute to consider whether your map will be item specific or time-specific. Do you want one or more maps for every situation?

2. Choose your main topic.

3. Complete your mapping.

Exercise 2 -- Create another mindmap for something else. Perhaps you have something to do with your shopping list, grocery list, or party list.

You might have noticed the shorter instructions for the exercises. This is because I want mind maps to be unique. They become something memorable and even more fun.

I'm interested in what you made. You can mail it to mailto

Goals Exercises

Now that you know what My Goals Mind Map looks and feels like, it's time for you to create your mind map. This is all about setting out your goals for life and then breaking them down into manageable pieces. Here are the two exercises.

Exercise 1: Make a Goals mindmap. You can only write down two to four goals in this exercise.

Main topic: Goals

Subtopics. What are you looking for? This can include any type of relationship, job, financial, or education. Write down only 2-4 goals.

Lower level topics: Break down the individual goals and make them smaller, more manageable.

Second level topics - Create actionable items for each lower topic. (If needed, further break down lower level topics and add actions items at a higher level.

Check your map, and make any needed changes.

Exercise 2 -- Redesign your Goals Map. Is there a way you could have done it differently

Exercise 3: Add the lower-level actions items to your To Do/Budget list maps.

I would like to see what you made. It can be sent by mailto:

Weight Loss Exercises

Let's do more. It was not about how to create a weight loss chart. You can skip exercising 1 and move on to exercise 2.

Exercise 1: Make a weight-loss map. You can make this as simple or complex as your heart desires.

Main topic – Weight loss

Add your subtopics.

You can embellish the piece by adding lines connecting to it.

Review - take the mindmap off for a couple of hours or even days before you go over it again. You can always go back to the map and change anything you think you forgot.

Exercise 2 - Pick a goal on your Goalsmap and map that goal out in details.

Exercise 3: Update your To Do List with any action items from exercises 1 or 2.

I am interested to see what you made. You can send it mailto:Maps

Purchase Exercises

The amount of choices available to us when we decide to buy something can be overwhelming and make it difficult for us to make the right decision. The solution is to mind map the choices.

Example of my purchase map for a new phone

Exemple of a new phone

Main topic: The New Phone

Subtopics: Cost and operating system, features. Brands. Service provider. Plans. And accident protection.

Exercise 1: Make a purchase list for the item that you are looking at buying.

Exercise 2 -- Is there a better, or different, way to organize your map from exercise 1? The map can be redone in another manner.

Shopping List Exercises

Make a shopping plan. This could include grocery aisles (meals, food groups), discounts, on-line or off-line purchases, and even shopping in stores. In Inspiration 9 software, add the cost to each item and then use the summation feature.

I organized mine by food categories, discounts, and rewards.

Exercise 1 - Create your shopping list. It doesn't have to be just for the grocery aisle.

Exercise 2 - Refresh your shopping cart with items that you have purchased and meals planned.

Meal Planning Exercises

Many ways can be used to plan meals. I prefer to plan all the meals for the entire week at once. This works well when I plan my weekly groceries.

Exercise 1: Plan out your meals.

Exercise 2- Redesign your meal plan so that you include the daily calories gained from weight loss. Inspiration 9 users - Add a summation of the totals for meals, weeks, and days to determine totals.

Chapter 12: Utilize Mind Maps

There are a few ways to make mindmaps that look both fundamental and extremely direct. However, these mind maps, which can seem tedious and tasteless, are actually quite stunning in their effectiveness. Psyche mapping is in fact very liberating and illuminating.

Work. It is incredible to see the number of people who don't know about psychemaps. When people talk about psyche guide and brain planning, it is common for them to be completely fresh. Even capturing and using data may not be something many people consider. This isn't something you do as a 'Regular' person. Many times, people with a lot of knowledge don't realize what a mental map is.

You can create your brain maps alone. However, if they don't work out for you, it is a good idea to share your thoughts with others. Show others what your brain maps have been like, how they have helped, and the reason you made them. You will make your friends, managers, supervisors and others see the value in this. You can and should help others in this way.

Mind planning is an effective tool for gaining a competitive advantage in the workplace. You can showcase your creativity, your plan aptitudes and your organization and hierarchical capabilities by introducing data through a mind guide. You might even be able to share some knowledge with others by simply outlining the issue on a psychemap.

You can run a meeting. Use a psychemap to guide you through a meeting. It can be used for imaginative apparatus, conceptualizing, critical thinking, or simply to demonstrate a point. Many people have grown so used seeing PowerPoint presentations, they are now more open to the idea of data being presented in a different and imaginative way.

Dozens of brain maps can be distributed before the event ends. This will enable people to better remember the topic of the gathering, and it will also drive your thoughts. The possibility of giving out duplicates may lead to people adding to the psyche manual. This will not only encourage investment, but it may lead to some innovative and valuable ideas that could assist you in reaching your goals.

When you have a gathering that uses a brainmap, why not make it more entertaining by handing out clear mental maps that everyone can use to look into what you have said. You can then ask them back at the end and order the data. This can be useful in helping you discover new ideas or help you resolve some issues. The likelihood of you receiving something in exchange for your efforts will be increased and the event will be more enjoyable.

Interview. The psyche mapping tool is something most people don't think of when meeting with prospective employees. This allows you to appear confident, focused, and steady. You can also use a mental guide to get data in meetings and to prepare your inquiries. This would be an opportunity to discuss how you routinely use mind planning for data gathering and presentation, as well to address issues. Most people will think that you are very bright, organized, and proactive. They can even support you.

Writing. Writing. This cycle works well regardless of how big or small the piece is. It is, in fact, the best instrument you can use to compose.

Use mind maps to organize your thoughts when you're writing books using bluff holders, pick-yourself books, or other types of books. Mind guides can be used by writers to arrange data and create multiple books with similar materials. It can be very helpful to include endnotes in your psyche-guide and to refer back to sources. This will help save you time later.

Networking. Mindmaps can also be used to help with system administration. Brain guides can improve your ability to communicate with others. It is possible to team up with people on the opposite end of the spectrum if you create a psyche diagram before you make a decision. This may help you or your gathering to collaborate better. Mind maps are fantastic for use in bunch settings, as they offer a method to draw individuals.

Social life. Mind guides can also be used to enhance public activity, something people often overlook. One remarkable example is the one where a man could see how people in his community knew each other. The game started as a fun one, but after some time, he was able use the knowledge to better understand people and their lives, which helped him to build his business. You could also use a brain map as a little book or business card holder. This would allow you to keep contact information from people groups and organize it according to what kind of relationship you have.

Shopping for gifts. A psychemap works well if you are trying to create a shopping checklist or a list full of blessings. This is a wonderful thing to do for any occasion that has many people involved, especially if it's a large purchase. This will assist you in monitoring what you have purchased as well as blessing thoughts and other items that your friends might like.

Romantic weekend. A brain guide would make it easy for anybody to create a meaningful end of the week. A brain guide would allow you to include the perfect contacts in your escape. However, your accomplice would be stunned by the care and detail you put into your plan. A brain guide could be used to ensure you don't run into any difficulties during your trip and help you get the best deal possible.

Planning a marriage. Organising a wedding is perhaps the most daunting task. It is the perfect opportunity to build a mental map. The time you are making the guest list is the best time to make a brainmap. This can be used as a reference point when sending out solicitations. It is possible to use a brainguide to see how much it will cost. You can save your cash by researching the cost for everything.

Designing your garden. If you love gardening, you probably have a lot of experience in designing gardens. You have to think about the seasons and plan your planting. To help you organize your arrangements, use a mental map or other brain guides. Keep adding or subtracting from them.

Life. A lot of people give up many important things in life because they aren't able to plan. Making arrangements will allow you to create your own life, instead of following every whim. For the best mind guides, make a point of using them every day. This will allow you to organize your life and help you achieve your goals. This helps to keep things in order and provides a method to address any issues that might arise. You will find it fun to do this daily. It helps you relax and let go of the pressure. You'll find it to be one of the most important things you do in your entire life.

Planning family events. Many people regret not investing their energy more effectively with their families. This goes back again to the earlier explanation about making life work, not allowing it. It is very difficult to let go of family and stop investing in it. If your family is important, you can use mind guides to continue to build your connections and find ways to get closer to each other.

Learning a foreign Language. This is another thing that everyone should once in a blue moon consider. To learn an unfamiliar language, you should use a brainmap. Working through a psyche book will aid you in recalling things, as has been stated. Electronic psyche map can be used to open and close the branches. If you are unsure whether or not you can use this ability to test it, simply indicate the word(s), then cover up the rest to see if they are there.

To learn more languages, you could branch them out. Italian is, for instance, very similar to Spanish. This means that you will be able to quickly master both languages by looking at both arrangements of jargon terms. To make it easier to associate data and organize the data better, you can even add pictures.

A budget is important. You can make a significant difference in your life and the lives of your family by planning your spending. The best part about psyche mapping is that they are constantly updated and become almost like a living report. This will enable you to keep an eye on what is due and where your cash is.

People often don't see the whole picture of how they are spending money until it is too late. Using a brainmap, you can look at the entire picture at once. A psyche planner can be helpful in planning for the future. It will help you to see what is coming and how to best contribute. You'll be more open to the possibility of missing out on opportunities, if you do this regularly.

You can use this tool to help you share your budgetary details with others. If you have a psychemap to help you monitor your finances, your mate and I can review it together towards the end of each month to determine what you need to do to improve your plans or put limitations where they are needed. Giving a brain guide to a financial professional or accountant can help them see more of your money situation. This will save time and help them make a better showing.

The first step in a new venture is to begin. One of the most terrifying things you can do is start another venture. Don't let fear stop you. You can't let this stop you. You can prepare to use a psychological guide to write your thoughts. Then, all things will turn out to less frightening.

Every arrangement that is made when you start another business can be carefully planned. Mind maps are useful for conceptualizing. You can use mind maps to arrange your costs, items, business associations, and so on. There are many formats that you can show to help with your business preparations. There are many combinations of brain maps that can be used to track your business and become more profitable.

You may be interested in trying something new. In this way, you can think up unique business ideas. Additionally, you can collect data as you test markets to see which ideas work best. To see how your loved ones perceive it, you can compile all of your thoughts and let them review it. Your brain map can be used to help you show how probable your thought is in order to prove that it is prone to delivering returns.

The great thing about brain mapping is that you can get both the material and the training. Through the process of creating a brainmap, you can think of innovative ideas, manage multiple factors, and solve problems. After your final steps, you will have an awesome record. This document clearly represents the culmination of all you have done. You have the ability to refer back to it or modify it.

The possible outcomes of planning this way are infinite. You might put some of the strategies discussed above to use. This is a suggested way to use mind mapping, but they are not the only option. These strategies will help you to discover new ways to use mind maps.

Chapter 13: Mind Mapping

Precautions

9 mind mapping misconceptions that beginners make. Here's how to stop them

Missing the point: Be obsessed with styling R

Your brain is not meant to be busy thinking about the content of your Brain Map. Instead, you need to spend time evaluating font dimensions. This is critical, but the graphic design process should be completed after the thought generations. This isn't just for mind mapping. Images and design are an important part of print design.

Consider switching between styling as well as the composing process. While task-hopping may give you a sense of accomplishment, it can also disrupt your thinking process. Studies have shown that short interruptions can lead to excess strain and productivity drops of around 40% in offices.

Option: Separation or content original

Content is the key. Everything else will follow. It is possible to keep your stress levels down by using topics and quick-styling if you can't seem to create a mental map. Xmind allows distraction-free mind mapping and provides the zen design, which means that only one headmap remains on your display.

Mistake number two: "perfectly" mind maps

Your mind map could take many forms and be large. You might feel that you are not getting enough quality and quantity of ideas when you start thinking about them. You may not be satisfied with the progress you make.

But "perfect" doesn't exist. You can only make great creations by shining. Shining is more than just polishing ideas. It also involves the types. Perfectionism in your mind mapping can be worse than weighing content over kind. Tony Buzan does have a lot of rules and guidelines for thinking maps, but many theories are found invalid. Many universities are encouraging students to "use them loosely" by publicly encouraging them.

Option: Accept your shitty initial draft

It is fine to have a fair first draft. Surprisingly, bloggers find it helpful. You can start to generate something original and your brain will be inspired by the job you do. You will be able to think more quickly if you have observable mindmaps. Scientists propose that the activity of mapping helps improve memory. Pre-constructed map, on the other side, do not help pupils learn.

Missing the mark 3: Too many clustering and confusing organizations

It is important to have a well-designed and detailed head map. However, your audience will be fine with it. It can obscure your overall arrangement and key factors.

Sometimes, it is not possible to be present before your viewers to walk them through and clarify their doubts. You cannot put your viewers at risk by creating a complicated, inept head map. Perplexing maps will not be able to be re-used for future reference even if you're the only person reading them.

Optional: organize using apparent visual clues

These are your top tips for organizing. Quick sanity checks could be as simple as looking at your maps after the task is completed. It shouldn't take more than two seconds to get to the main stage and construction.

Bruce Wong from Xmind is a senior item director. Here is an example from his mindmap collection.

Missing 4: Your demonstration seems too rigid

Head maps, unlike linear tracks, can engage the viewer more in casual demonstrations. However, when mind-mappers first begin to create mind maps, they tend to produce extremely boring ones. Fun-seekers are always looking for excitement and stimulation.

Option: Have your brain maps created and available for you to live

Many attributes can be added to applications to make your maps more dynamic. An easy way to make an interesting graph is to include gifs and coloured branches. Your viewers will focus more on certain sections if you break down a chapter. You can engage more viewers during your demonstration by inserting attachment documents, such sound and video in your diagrams.

Mistake 5? You rely entirely on your head maps

What is mind mapping? A mind map is a tree diagram with a central motif. Mind maps have their limitations, but not everyone can. The brain map is one of many tools. To communicate your thoughts effectively, your brain map is only one tool.

Option: Merge your brainmaps with other programs

Xmind supports various export formats, which can help users connect to other applications. Mind maps can be placed within Evernote in an outline or as a creative article for an in-depth information map. You can use it as part of your google slide.

Mistake 6: missing in details

Your thoughts can grow. They can become overwhelming and you may get lost. Brainstorming does not work if everyone has constructive and applicable insight. Information is often more static than notes and infographics. Keep in mind that the mind map is a boat. If you stuff your mind map with random ideas it can be likened to a jar containing sauce and other components. It may provide some serendipity. However, it's still drifting away from your initial goals.

Option: Write down what your goal is

Yes. It's quite simple. You can place your goal on top of the map. Alternately you can write it down and place the item somewhere that you are able to clearly see. Visually examining your goal will help your mind recall it.

Failure 7: Insistence production, but not forced

It may seem like forced creation has created a habit of inventing, but you don't feel the need to repeat yourself. If you find yourself making the same thought maps as you did yesterday, it might be worth challenging yourself. The challenge extends beyond visual layout to include comprehension of advice or special ideas.

Optional: Replicate the seasoned

Your most efficient way of succeeding is to copy masters. Duplicating is inherently bad. Twyla Tharp (mythical inventive artist) disagrees. She describes her key to imagination as being "busy copiing" in her best-selling publication, The Deadly Habit. She believes "following the footprints of someone else is a very important method of learning a skill." Platforms like mindmap gallery, biggerplate and other communities are filled with inspiration. It might be simpler to hunt for mind maps in the topic-specific communities cardano education and freecodecamp.

Make 8: Maps are not for you

Mind mapping is a great tool for self-reflection. But keeping it to yourself limits its potential benefits. Complex problem solving requires knowledge from many parties. But don't endanger your self-contemplation. Otherwise, category wisdom can become groupthink.

Option: Share and Collaborate Groups

University of York researchers have tested three kinds of collaborations. Learning can be greatly enhanced by dispersed collaboration.

It is necessary for the group to agree on the arrangements of editors and editing. A map editor can only edit one map. Others may view the previous map version before the present editor publishes their variation and passes to another member. The team performs well because they integrate self-contemplation with collective wisdom. Xmind provides several methods for mind mapping dispersed collaboration.

Mistake 9

Perhaps you're inclined to think that mind mapping is only for creative work after having read some reports or sites. Research has shown that brain maps can also help with more organized topics like patent legislation, chemical technology, or medical science. Awareness is the foundation of commonality.

Option: Create mind maps for "not-suitable" areas

Make a list and try to map your brain to the areas that aren't possible.

Actions

To sum up:

Original content, separation from concerns

Accept your first draft.

Organize using apparent visual cues

Get your brain maps to live

Use different resources to combine your brainmaps

Write down your goal

Copy the seasoned

Collaborate and Share groups

Use mind mappings across topics

5 reasons not to mind map

1. You can either stop mind-mapping once you reach your goal (or you find the solution).

This is why you should stop mind mapping. The map served its purpose. The goal was achieved, the answer was discovered, the catastrophe was avoided, you won, anyway...

Most people give up on creating their mind maps. This is a common reason for beginners to quit. They stop before becoming successful. Unusual? Perhaps, but the message is clear.

2. The situation or problem is known.

You have come across a difficult situation. This could be on the job, in a personal crisis, or just something that you don't understand. What should you do instead? The best thing is to create a mindmap.

3. A better way of finding a response was found

Hey... It's okay to use a different strategy when it is better. It could be that you have another tool or a man to help. If that is true, ensure that you don't remain stuck on your head map. Accept the new prospect.

Your mind map should be kept in place. You don't know what another person might want to know about your progress or insights. Even if the instrument or person you have chosen is not for you, you can always go back to where your started.

Many people find that mind maps are not what they need. A mind map might be the best resource they could use, so they start to use it. They use a mind map for example to keep their schedule on track. What are their real jobs? They create a map with branches. The branches are known as Monday Tuesday Wednesday etc. Indeed??? Yes.

It is essential to be objective when creating a mind map.

4. The map's function is complete and the benefits are no longer provided by it

You know what? It can be done quickly with mind mapping ideas. A brain map is simply one more method of studying the exact same information. A lot of times, when you look at a sheet, you might just find the insight that you are looking for.

A clear perspective can be achieved by simply drawing a picture of a problem, target, or circumstance and placing it on a plan. Sometimes, the simplest outline can be enough to give you clarity that it will allow you to arrive at the answer.

It's crucial to stop working on the map after reaching your destination.

A quick tip: It isn't on the map. A brainmap is only a tool. Sometimes, mind mapping is used to eliminate the target. They can create a much more stunning map, with many colors and graphics. They spend way too much time looking at the maps and not on the actual purpose of having a brainmap. This is what you need to keep in mind.

You should not be focusing on mapping when the goal is not being met.

5. After the map is ruined

Sometimes it's enough to realize that a map isn't working for you. There may be several reasons.

Too much emphasis on material rather than the map

Focusing only on the wrong topics

Too many branches make it difficult to see the map.

The map is too large. It has many details.

The data isn't organized properly

If this happens, you must act fast. You need to find the problem and then fix it.

Do not waste your time on a poorly functioning map. You have more important things to do.

It's now time to do this and maybe stop brain mapping

These activity points can help you assess whether your brain map needs to be updated or not.

Action point 1 - Every day that you start mind mapping look at it and ask yourself if this is the best tool. Is it the best thing for me? Change procedures if necessary.

Action point two: Different avenues produce various insights. This map can be modified to provide a fresh understanding and new ways of approaching a problem. Ask a friend if they can inspect the map. They will then give you their findings and create a new version.

Action point 3. Request a brain mapping professional to look at your map. I am often presented with maps by my customers that do nothing to help them progress. It is often possible to see the big picture and make some significant changes that will help you achieve success.

Action 4: Get a brain mapping tool if you're not already.

Mind maps help prevent head fracture

You may even forget what keywords you are if you concentrate on one term for more then 3 minutes. If you focus on one thing too much, you may forget what it is and what you have. Sometimes, your memory may trap you into believing that you have more knowledge than you actually are. You can then conquer your mind, but nothing comes up. Each scenario shows fragmentation. Many people wonder if they can find a tool to improve their memory and prevent fragmentation. The answer is yes. It is a Brain Map. You can use it to create a brainstorm or join your thoughts in order boost your memory. The next section will explain how to prevent mind fragmentation by using thought maps.

#StimulatetheBrain

Mind maps can inspire your mind by using colorful icons and clip art. Mind maps can be more focused than the simplex liner notes. They are also shorter and easier to read. Drawings should contain at least three bright colors for those who prefer to think but not be stressed. You can use icons and symbols to help highlight and differentiate the various parts of your brain maps. Mind maps are more fun when they can be merged into a picture.

Build construction of your head

Mind maps make mind construction easier and more logical. Brainstorming is easier when you are in a relaxed state. Mind mapping allows you to explore your thoughts deeply and create a list of your thoughts. The whole process can be described as divergent modes of thinking that are free from any restriction. Other methods, like notes from speeches or presentations, can be hard to remember and examine.

repeat

Drawing a brainmap is a way to repeat a procedure. Repeating is key to memorizing, as you likely know. A brain map's branch can be explained using a variety of colours, tags or icons. You will make a profound impression about this part by using photographs, tags, icons, icons, and other visuals. The shapes and lines you see in the next branch will change when you draw it. The practice of replicating is meant to strengthen each component in your brain. The entire headmap is also in one newspaper. Therefore, you can look for it alongside your current drawing. Even better, the design will give users lots of memories. This allows you to slow down the process of transforming unconsciousness into consciousness.

#model that offers a holistic view

Mind maps help you build a habit of linking colours, images, key words, thoughts, and other concepts together. Mind maps are a great way to reduce the traditional mindset. Traditional thinking trains inductive capability. Mind mapping will not only help you understand inductive capability, but also provide divergent, advanced evaluation abilities. To recreate the holistic view of your entire mind map, drill and stop.

Mind mapping tools help to unify thoughts from different sources and bring them together into a single net. Methodical thinkers will be the end result. You can prevent mind fragmentation by using brain mapping tools to map your head.

Conclusion

Mind maps are very powerful tools that you can use to study, solve problems and take notes. They allow you to unleash your creative mind and use it to solve problems, make decisions, improve your memory and increase your ability to remember.

With some pens and a piece blank (not lined), paper, you can create a mindmap. This is referred to as a landscape layout. You should have the long edge at your top. The main idea you are mind-mapping is written at the center of your page. You should use large fonts and capital letters for this. If you would prefer to include an illustration, that is also possible. You might also want to draw an outline of the central concept in a color circle.

This central concept will serve as the basis for your chapter headings. The next most important concepts in relation to the central idea. These can also appear in capital letters. These connections are made by connecting them to the main idea with a thick and large line. This is to indicate the importance.

These can be used to hang off a third level of concepts.

You can use colors, shapes and photos to help create a visual mind map that stimulates your brain. It will also help you remember everything.

Mind maps work well as mnemonics if you need to quickly recall information from a seminar, book or meeting. It helps you remember the information not only later but also at any other time.

If you have to make a decision or solve an issue, then this mindmap can be a useful tool. The mindmap allows you to organize and visualize the information, so that your brain can take it in, or use it to create a solution.

Some people prefer to use software, while other prefer to make their mind maps by hand. It is up to you whether you prefer to draw one with a pencil or use a computer. Each method has its advantages and disadvantages. It's up to you how you prefer to work.

Mind maps can be helpful for anyone, whether they are students or professionals who need to retain information.

Mind maps are extremely useful tools to assist with problem solving and recall. You can use them anywhere and unleash the creative potential of your mind. The diagrams allow you to use all aspects of your mind when you are working with words, colors and images. Diagrams enable you to connect the dots between various concepts and jumps of judgement or knowledge.

No matter what profession you choose, you'll find mind maps very useful. They help you remember facts as well as solve problems. The ability to use mind mappings can make a significant difference to your recall and learning to study. This is something that you will be able to benefit from.

www.ingramcontent.com/pod-product-compliance
Lightning Source LLC
Chambersburg PA
CBHW071845080526
44589CB00012B/1117